Hypnosis, Relaxation and Suggestion from a CBT Perspective

NILS NORRSELL

Hypnosis, Relaxation and Suggestion from a CBT Perspective

Handbook for clinicians, especially within dentistry

© 2018 Nils Norrsell
Layout: BoD – Books on Demand
Printing: BoD – Books on Demand, Stockholm, Sweden
Production: BoD – Books on Demand, Norderstedt, Germany
ISBN: 978-91-7785-301-5

Contents

Introduction

The word hypnosis has to do with sleep. Deep relaxation sometimes can be experienced as a form of sleep, but the word hypnosis is not optimal, as clinical hypnosis in general is more like a waking state with a sense of deep relaxation and calmness. Due to lack of a better name the word hypnosis is still in use. There has been different names during different times. In the antiquity the state was called temple sleep, at the end of the 1800th century the name mesmerism or animal magnetism were used. Today much focus is on mindfulness and meditation, that can be seen as variants of hypnosis. A common name for these mental states is an altered state of consciousness (ASC). This means that it is different than the ordinary waking mental state.

Hypnosis can be a great help for many patients in dentistry and medical treatment, in fact for the majority. The primary aim is often relaxation. With the right technique this can be achieved within a couple of well used minutes. The treatment will be well tolerated, the patient will be more content and happy and for the caregiver the job satisfaction will increase. Many patients will learn to relax automatically during treatment.

Even if the induction technique may be easy to learn, hypnosis is a comprehensive subject calling for great engagement for a successful practise. After induction it is important to know how to maintain and use the altered mental state in the best way. The combination of hypnosis and

Cognitive behaviour therapy (CBT), will make teaching of new behaviours, including relaxation, very effective.

Problems that the patients often need help with are phobia of different things inclusive pain and needles, exaggerated gagging reflexes, bruxism, motivation for dental care and also health promoting behaviours in general like stress management and smoking cessation. This book has two principal aims. One is to promote understanding of theories behind hypnosis and suggestion together with treating principals, collected mainly from CBT. Another is to teach suitable relaxation induction techniques and inspire dental and health caregivers to study and use hypnosis and suggestion in their working field.

Practitioners that don't see any possibilities to influence patients showing signs of tension and suffering often disregard such signs or belittle them. That can initiate a life lasting phobia. Hypnosis gives great possibilities to influence. Observation skills are basic when practising hypnosis, and the insight that you can help patients with problem behaviours facilitates to observe them and to take them into account. It calls for a little extra from the care provider, but with the right knowledge and willingness to help the reward in the form of grateful patients will be rich.

No extraordinary gift is required to become a good hypnotist. It is enough to be interested, to be willing to put the patient in the center, and to be receptive to his or her needs. There is a lot of interesting literature on hypnosis and related subjects. To study this and also some video demonstrations on the internet is recommended. Of course it is of great importance to get an approved education, to practise and to learn by observing other professionals.

As a beginner you should take all opportunities to practise in order to gain confidence. Within dentistry I recommend the use of the standard induction that I have elaborated and used for 40 years with small variations. It is quick, you must not think of how to start and it has the necessary ingredients to reach your goals. It is well suited for the clinical environment where you want to evoke a scientific and professional image of yourself. From the patient's responses you will understand how well your induction has succeeded and with practice you will get skilled.

CBT deals with learned responses, unlearning of negative reflexes and behaviours and learning of new, more appropriate ones. I divide thought responses and body responses into two categories, reflexes and behaviours. That is different from the current view, but it facilitates the understanding. The combination of hypnosis and CBT is so effective that it alone could help the majority of those phobic patients, who are today relying on expensive general anesthesia or nitrous oxide.

Everybody knows the fact that tension can be built up in seconds, but it is not so well known that relaxation can be triggered as quickly. Well-tried and effective methods for helping suffering patients in clinical settings are described and explained.

1. Development of hypnosis

Within medicine hypnosis surely is as old as the art of healing itself. It is a special state of consciousness which during the antiquity was called temple sleep. This indicates that striking similarities with ordinary sleep were observed. This special state of consciousness was noted at the end of the 18th century by Franz Anton Mesmer (1734-1815) in Vienna. He was influenced by the scientific discovery of magnetism in metals and believed that there was magnetic radiation in the cosmos, emanating from the stars. He imagined that it was possible to magnetize living creatures by stroking and called it animal magnetism. His belief came from the observation that his patients, after persistent stroking went into a dormant rest, a kind of daze. At the time it was difficult to find a better explanation than magnetism.

Some of the patients reacted by getting excited and going into convulsions when they were assembled round a reportedly magnetized tub. It contained iron filings connected to metal bars which the patients were instructed to hold. Strong expectation reigned and the atmosphere was supported by glas harmonica music. Naturally the participants influenced each other's expectations and feelings. The tension grew and resulted in convulsions that spread from one person to another. Mesmer talked about beneficent crises that he regarded as health bringing cures.

James Esdaile (1808–1859) was a British surgeon who worked in India using animal magnetism as the only anaesthetic agent until the 1840s when nitrous oxide (laughing gas) was shown to be effective. Another doctor in Scotland, James Braid (1795-1860), became interested in the method but rejected the theory of magnetism. He considered the mental state to be a kind of sleep and first used the term hypnotism. Later he resented this but it was to late because the notion had already been established but was later altered to hypnosis.

The French doctor Jean-Martin Charcot (1825-1893) saw hypnotizability as an inborn quality and sign of a hysteric disposition. His colleges Ambroise-Auguste Liébeault (1823-1904) and Hippolyte Bernheim (1840- 1919) on the other hand saw hypnosis as an effect of suggestion. In Germany the neurologist Oscar Vogt (1870-1959) worked successfully with hypnosis. His pupil, Johannes Heinrich Schultz became interested in what deeply hypnotized people experienced. Most of them felt heaviness in the arms, warmth in the hands and reported slow, calm breathing. Schultz developed Autogenic Training when he realized that self-hypnosis could be induced merely by focusing on these fenomena by silently repeating the words for them. The method is popular in Germany.

Charcot's pupil, Sigmund Freud (1856-1939), became famous. He abandoned hypnosis and, theorist as he was, founded psychoanalysis. The method builds on free associations and interpretation of dreams. Sexuality was considered to be the most important psychological drive. The part of the unconscious craving for immediate satisfaction of a need, Freud called the Id. The part of the psyche occupied with making choices, good in the long run he called the Ego. The part, occupied with social norms he called the Super Ego. Sexual abuse and internal conflict were seen as main causes of psychological illness.

Josef Breuer, another of Charcot's pupils took in the beginning part of the development of psychoanalytical theory but then went his own way. He was a clever clinician and had great success as a hypnotherapist. He noticed that neurotic symptoms could disappear when the causes, sited to the unconscious had become conscious.

The Frenchman Pierre Janet (1859-1947), also educated by Charcot, worked like his master with hysteria. He developed the important theory of dissociation. It says that the consciousness can be divided into different parts, totally unaware of each other. Janet observed that such a split often happens spontaneously after traumatic experiences.

Research indicates there may be an inborn ability to protect the organism against emotional overload. It was called the relaxation response by Herbert Benson (1935-) This response can be triggered voluntarily in meditation. Some memories are state bound and appear only when a certain feelings are evoked. Ernest Hilgard (1904 – 2001) showed that dissociation can be induced in ordinary healthy peoples. It is an important mechanism in hypnotic pain control.

Emile Coué (1857-1926) was trained by the famous Dr. Auguste Liebault (1823-1904) in Nancy. He learned a lot both from Liebault and his eminent pupil Hippolyte Bernheim (1840-1919). Coué, however, had an objection to his teachers woking methods. He meant that hypnosis was not perceived as a sleeping state by everyone and therefore he used only the notions suggestion and autosuggestion with the patient in a waking state. Aaron Beck (1921-), the founder of cognitive therapy in the 1960s, found that in the treatment of depression systematic shifting from negative thoughts to more positive, but still realistic ones was effective.

In USA a hypnotist named Phineas Quimby (1802-1866) cured an unhealthy woman Mary Baker Eddy (1821-1910) in the middle of the 19th century. She was very imposed, but rejected hypnosis but founded the religion Christian Science, mainly built on ideas from her experiences of the power of suggestion. She meant that faith in God, positive thinking and denial of the existence of illness was important for health. She saw illnesses as delusions that would disappear if you refused to believe in them and told yourself that man is an image of God and thus healthy.

After the two world wars hypnosis got an upswing, as it was shown that it was effective in the treatment of shock. Dentists became interested and found hypnosis effective in treatment of dental phobia and many of the associated problems like muscular tension, hypersensitivity to pain and gagging.

One of the most renowned within hypnosis is the American Milton Erickson (1901-1980). His pupil, the dentist Kay Thompson (1930-1998) has contributed to increased knowledge of hypnosis in dentistry. Another American, Dave Elman (1900-1969) has launched many effective induction methods that suit well into the clinical setting of dentistry and medicine as they focus on relaxation and anesthesia.

An important discovery, made by Milton Erickson as a teenager was when he, paralyzed by polio and not able to move his arms consciously, found that he could influence them by focusing on a certain goal and thus trigger muscle reflexes. When his hand lay immobile, despite his strong wish to reach a pencil lying close to it, he was amazed when he noticed a little movement towards the pencil. He understood that muscles can be influenced not only by willpower, but also by intense imagination that triggers reflexes. (p. 47, ideomotor effect).

Hypnosis in dentistry
Hypnosis has been used by dentists since late 1900th century. In an American newspaper from that time there was a report about a demonstration of hypnosis for dentists. Everybody had been imposed and it was believed that within a few years the majority of dentists would use hypnosis. Unfortunately it turned out not to be the case. The interest has fluctuated over the years.

In the beginning great importance was attached to the possibility to create anesthesia without chemicals. Hypnosis was also used to reduce vomiting reflexes, bleeding and to help patients to tolerate dentures. All these things are good, but nowadays the main focus has shifted to treatment of dental fear that is often connected to the above mentioned problems. Another treatment, that seems to get ever increased importance is the treatment of bruxism, a contemporary, serious, stress related problem.

The new occupational group, dental hygienist, could make an important contribution in helping their patients by learning how to use hypnosis for relaxation and for treatment of bruxism. The knowledge of hypnosis has grown internationally and Cognitive Behaviour Therapy (CBT) has contributed to the understanding of how anxiety problems can be dealt with in an effective way. The best and quickest results are gained if not only CBT but also hypnosis is used as shown by Kirsch (1995). The aim of this book is to reveal in a logic manner how hypnosis combined with CBT can be used in dental and medical practice. Hypnosis is a very effective method for relaxation that is needed for desensitizing (making less sensible) to anxiety provoking stimuli.

For people working in the field of dentistry or medicine the study of positive psychology can be recommended. The same methods that can help people in therapy can be used for those who just want to optimize their quality of life. It is about self-awareness, positive thinking, relaxation, hypnosis, meditation, exercise and other health promoting behaviours.

2. The origin and frequency of dental fear

The attitude of a new patient to dental care is characterized by past experiences. The previous experiences are not always representative of normal dental treatment, but have become a model for all dental care. It becomes a kind of false, outdated inner map that underlies the existing negative expectations. If dental treatment has been avoided or the skewed image has been enhanced by further negative experiences the possibility to update the map has been lacking. The patient then continues to see a series of threats on his/her inner map.

All humans create a mental representation of the world we live in. We make an image of how reality is thought to be. It's a kind of model that is needed to orient oneself safely. It does not be particularly detailed, but it should be as close as possible to the reality. Therefore it needs to be updated from time to time. A common cause of error is that general conclusions are drawn from single events. A single pain experience during dental treatment can lay the ground for a pain phobia.

Despite modern methods of treatment, about 2- 5% of people in the western countries feel so much discomfort that they avoid dental care completely. Relatively big discomfort is felt by about 50% of the population or more. Much can be done to reduce the discomfort. Among the most important is to make tense patients relax and to avoid working on them until they have relaxed. The right kind of treatment allows updating of the inner map and taking away many false warning signs.

Those based on events that will definitely no longer occur should be sorted out directly. To these belong negative images of the child being hold by force. Such an event, even if short in time, may result in a lifelong feeling of threat. The initial memory should then be supplemented with a reality based view of what kind of treatment an adult could I expect from a caregiver using hypnosis. It is giving the patient full control and under no circumstances carry out holding by force.

Earlier negative experiences are often the cause of discomfort when going to dental hygienist or dentist. Anxiety reflexes, which can not be directly affected by the will, may be a concern. There is often an excessive negative interpretation of different stimuli, such as noise, vibration, negative visual impressions, etc. This results in both conscious and unconscious muscle tension that enhances discomfort, which in turn can lead to total avoidance. The longer a person has avoided dental care due to fear or other negative feelings, the stronger their negative beliefs will be. One could say that they easily enter a negative feeling supported by threatening fantasies, a kind of negative self-hypnosis.

In CBT, one talks about automatic negative thoughts. With the help of the Dental Fear Survey (DFS) below, you can get an idea of what they look like, the physiological responses and what triggers. Fear at level 5 In the form below indicates a severe phobia. This does not mean, however, that it must be difficult to treat, only that it has serious consequences for the victim. Avoidance behaviour leads to long periods without dental care, failure to arrive at an appointment and risk of reinforcement of negative perception, when care is only sought in emergency situations.

People are different in terms of sensitivity already from birth. This is well described in the book HSP – The Highly Sensitive Person by Elaine Aron.

In CBT one talks about different vulnerability. Theoretically it could be about an inborn high suggestibility. For babies who get the right help with emotional regulation this could be an advantage. If no help is available, the sensitivity will make anxiety get too big proportions. The important attachment to a caregiver during the first year in life will be damaged or lacking. According to John Bowlby this is the cause of many psychiatric problems.

A dentist or dental hygienist is not supposed to give psychological treatment. To teach relaxation is however nothing more than a behavioural influence that is helpful for a majority of dental patients, including those with psychiatric diagnosis. When you have a patient with a known diagnosis of schizophrenia, be careful not to evoke harmful fantasies. Work with relaxation only. In CBT progressive relaxation, according to Jacobson, has been used a lot since the days of Wolpe in the middle of the 20th century.

Dental Fear Survey   (Originator: Kleinknecht 1977)

Name...................................   Date..

Please circle the number of the category which most closely corresponds to your reaction.

1. Has fear of dental work ever caused you to put off making an appointment?

1	2	3	4	5
never	once or twice	a few times	often	nearly every time

2. Has fear of dental work ever caused you to cancel or not appear for an appointment?

1	2	3	4	5
never	once or twice	a few times	often	nearly every time

When having dental work done:
3. My muscles become tense...

1	2	3	4	5
not at all	a little	noticable	much	very much

4. my breathing rate increases...

1	2	3	4	5
not at all	a little	noticable	much	very much

5. I perspire...

1	2	3	4	5
not at all	a little	noticable	much	very much

6. I feel nausated and sick to my stomach...

1	2	3	4	5
not at all	a little	noticable	much	very much

7. My heart beats faster...

1	2	3	4	5
not at all	a little	noticable	much	very much

Please rate how much fear, anxiety or unpleasantness the items below cause you. Scale 1-5 like above.

8. Making an appointment for dentistry...
9. Approaching the dentists office....
10. Sitting in the waiting room.....
11. Being seated in the dental chair.....
12. The smell of the dentist's office....
13. Seeing the dentilt walk in.....
14. Seeing the anesthetic needle.....
15. Feeling the needle injected.....
16. Seeing the drill....
17. Hearing the drill....
18. Feeling vibrations from the drill.....
19. Having your teeth cleaned.....
20. All things considered, how fearful are you of having dental work done?.........

For the assessment of tension and dental fear, the DFS form is recommended. It provides an overview of both avoidance and it's frequency, physiological stress symptoms, which stimuli arouse discomfort and how strong it is. Relaxation is something patients can learn. In CBT you can use "applied relaxation" according to Öst. For those who work with hypnosis, it may be good to know this way of teaching a patient to relax. Great emphasis is put on the person's ability to relax on his own. The method is about alternatively tense and relax different muscles to feel the difference.

Individual exercise is done twice a day and on the special form the result is reported. Once it has been satisfactory, the procedure will be shortened until the patient is able to master rapid relaxation based on conditioning. Relaxation can then be triggered by just taking a deep breath and focusing on the feeling of relaxation when exhaling. With hypnotic techniques the result will be considerably enhanced.

Another relaxation method, autogenic training, was launched in the early 20th century by I. H. Schultz. He was a student of the German Professor Oscar Vogt and became curious about what the subjects experienced when they were in deep hypnosis. Through interviews he found that they often experienced weight in their arms, warmth in their hands and calm breathing. He could then show the subjects that they could develop the hypnotic state themselves by repeatedly saying or thinking the words: the arms are heavy, the hands are hot, my breathing is calm, etc. The method has been used extensively in Germany and has been taught systematically to up to one hundred people at a time.

In order to become aware of one's tension level, it may be good to occasionally try to assess where it is on the scale 1-100 where 100 represents 100%. Since tension and relaxation are forces, regulated by the sympathetic and the parasympathetic nerve systems, antagonistic to each other, the level of 50 can be seen as normal tension. At levels under 50 the relaxation dominates and over 50 excitement, engagement or tension dominate. If tension is unnecessarily high, it is good if it can be quickly lowered.

The operator who works with hypnosis can help patients to relax, but in some cases it may be good for the patient to practice relaxation on his own. Those who are overly tense and have trained to release a conditioned relaxation response by just taking a deep breath can use this many times a day in situations that tend to increase stress. For documentation of practice, the registration form on the next page is suitable.

Interesting facts about the Relaxation Response have been demonstrated by Herbert Benson. It can be triggered by Transcendental Meditation, TM, Autogenic Training, Hypnosis with suggestions of deep relaxation and several other techniques He found that TM meditators, just by the simple technique of repeating a word or a sound, evoke a parasympathetic response of relaxation in just a couple of minutes. This results in a mental state, characterized by alpha waves in the brain and body relaxation combined with low oxygen consumption. Regular training has great health effects.

RECORD CARD OF DAILY RELAXATION TRAINING

Namn:..

Tension is graduated on a scale 1-100 where 100 represents max. tension and normal tension is 50. Everything under 50 means that relaxation dominates over tension.

Date and time.	Tension before	Tension after	Minutes	Comments

3. Classical conditioning. Odontological views

In a classical experiment by the Russian physiologist Ivan Pavlov (1849-1936), he investigated how salivary secretion was affected in dogs. A tuning fork was struck immediately before food was placed in the mouth. The sound, which from the beginning was a neutral stimulus, soon became associated with food. It turned out that saliva secretion increased when the sound of the tuning fork was heard, even though no food was placed in the mouth. The secretion increased the more times the sound was presented together with food up to a certain limit. This means that two stimuli, presented simultaneously are associated with each other, so called classical conditioning. The food is an unconditioned stimulus, the sound is a conditioned one. The autonomic nervous system responds to a conditioned stimulus in the same way as the unconditioned stimulus to which the signal was originally associated.

An early, famous experiment
with classic condition was made by John B. Watson around 1920. Watson first showed that his experimental subject, a 9 month child named Albert, had no initial fear of a domestic white rat. His reaction was a little curiosity. Watson had previously shown that sharp sound induces horror signs like trembling and crying in small children. Knowing this he could test the theory of conditioning by using a sharp sound as unconditioned stimulus and the white rat as a conditioned stimulus. Just as the white rat was presented, someone hit a steel bar behind the boy's head so that

a sharp, unpleasant sound was generated. After several such repetitions, Albert started crying and showing other signs of fear as soon as he saw the white rabbit without the sound being heard. Eventually, he was afraid of everything that was hairy. This phenomenon is called generalization and is common in phobias.

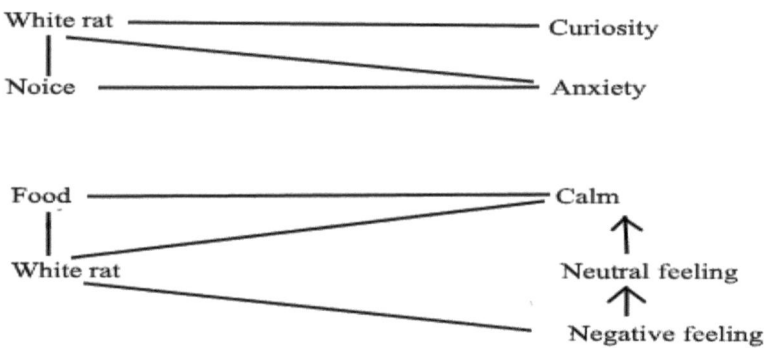

Fig 1. Schematic presentation of the theory of desensitization in the case of Albert.

Classical conditioning is learning by association of simultaneously experienced stimuli and by associating them to the emotion of the moment. A clear example of this is that the drilling and the drilling sound occur simultaneously with pain and therefore they become associated with each other so that they later trigger the same anxiety reflex in the autonomic nerve system (see Figure 1). As the reflex once was learned it can be influenced by new learning. By first evoking an emotion of calm and then gradually presenting the stimulus (drilling sound) that you want to be conditioned to the calm feeling, relearning takes place. However, the earlier conditioned emotion can later come back without visible reason (spontaneous recovery). That means that people who have been desensitized and cured from a phobia are more prone to get the same phobia than others.

Interesting experiments with classical conditioning can be made with a so-called polygraph. It measures the electrical conductivity of the skin and can be used as a lie detector. Conductivity drops for a few seconds (electrodermal response (EDR)) if we get scared or if we lie. The device was used extensively by various companies in the United States during the 1950s to test employee loyalty. The abuse became so great that such use was prohibited.

The noise of a running drill easily becomes a conditioned negative stimulus as it is often combined with pain and discomfort. The appearance of probes and syringes can similarly trigger discomfort by reminding of previous unpleasant visits to a dentist or dental hygienist. Words can also be conditioned stimuli. In the 1920s and 1930s, "nation" and "socialism" were generally associated with something positive. Hitler used these words and called his party the National Socialist German Workers Party.

In a dental or medical clinic it is advisable to avoid certain words that may adversely affect the patient. Such words are e.g. " bad, long needle, pain, dangerous, hurt, spray, drill, bloody, risk, hard." It is totally meaningless to say to a scared child that "it does not hurt" or "it's not dangerous", because what the child notices are the words corresponding to its actual feeling.

Some smells may be associated with discomfort. Of course, you can not know and avoid every distressing stimuli, but some are quite obvious. As for others, observation of the patient's responses may give a clue to what is alarming. For some, air blasting is a negative stimulus whether or not the teeth are anesthetised. For others, it may be a stimulus as innocent as a wheezing suction, a probe or wrapping the napkin chain around the neck that causes a negative emotion.

Many actions by dentists, and certainly also of hygienists may be perceived as threat signals. They put the organism into an alarm condition by secretion of adrenaline in the blood stream. It has been shown that merely lightening of the operation illumination may cause a stress reaction. The sight of a syringe, dental pliers or a scalpel obviously may be frightening. When it comes to giving injections it's often recommendable, especially with children, not to remove the protective cap until it is in the mouth. It is very rare that a child responds negatively to this procedure if the atmosphere is calm.

Of course, you should never lie and say there is no needle. If anyone is wondering, just tell the truth, that you want to try out where to put the anesthesia and to give an idea of what it is felt like. You could also offer a little anesthetic ointment on the hood and press it toward the place where you want to inject. It is explained that giving the anesthesia usually feels like a weak pressure. The hood is gently removed and the injection is administered slowly. Words like careful, numbing drops, light, pressure, gently and slowly should be used. Of course, it is important that the operator is calm and striving to give painless injections, which is an art in itself.

How the patient is spared unnecessary anxiety
The best is of course if unfavorable conditioning is prevented. Therefore, you should always perform treatment, especially of children, as painless as possible. This does not mean that you must dependent on chemical anesthesia, as pain relief can be achieved through hypnosis. The first time a little child visits a dental care center, it should be given the opportunity to get acquainted with the equipment and maybe to play with angle piece, drill, spray, blister, suction, etc.

In cases where the patient has already a conditioned fear or anxiety, any stimuli that may be anxiety-inducing should be removed if possible. Syringes should never be seen in the patient's field of vision. Blood splash may not be present. Drill stands should preferably not be placed in front of the patient's eyes. These should preferably be closed during treatment, even in cases where you have not planned to use hypnosis. Beneficial trance will often occur spontaneously, especially in patients, used to hypnosis.

Generalization

As mentioned before, generalization occurs of conditioned fear. Therefore, the entire environment in a dental clinic may be scaring to phobic patients. In the case of Albert, the therapy consisted of placing the white rat, of which he was afraid, in the corner of the room while he was eating. Eating was considered incompatible with fear. The following days the rat was placed closer and closer to the little boy. This was done so gradually that the fear of the rat finally disappeared. The procedure is called successive approximation.

Psychotherapy through reciprocal inhibition and desensitization.

Joseph Wolpe has developed a method of treating conditioned, i.e. learned anxiety responses. He called the method psychotherapy through reciprocal inhibition. It is similar to the method used in Albert's case. Instead of food, Wolpe uses relaxation, which like eating, is considered incompatible with anxiety. Treatment consists of making a list of fear provoking stimuli, graded from the least to the most fearful. In a relaxed state the patient is given the task to imagine them all, one by one until no anxiety is elicited even by the most anxiety provoking stimuli on the list. This is called desensitization. Relaxation must be present throughout the procedure for reciprocal inhibition to work.

4. Desensitization in dentistry

The following steps are applied:

1. The form Dental Fear Survey, DFS, is filled out by the patient.
2. An interview about the fear is made and in most cases the patient remembers how it started. The planned treatment is described in order to calm the patient. The theory of desensitization is explained and the importance of relaxation is emphasized.
3. Hypnosis is used to achieve maximal relaxation.
4. The therapist suggests finger levitation as a signal of being prepared to keep the relaxation while the feared stimulus is presented in a safe way. As long as relaxation remains unaffected the finger should be up, but if tension is felt the finger should be lowered immediately. Then relaxation should be regained and the training has to take one step back. Sound from the high speed angel piece often triggers fear. The presentation of the sound should be made from a long distance for a second or two. Then the time should be extended and the distance gradually diminished. The exercise should continued until it is possible to run the highspeed inside the mouth with sustained relaxation and without discomfort. The whole procedure usually takes only ten minutes.

The method can be seen as desensitization in vivo. It allows you to treat fear of drilling noise and vibration, needles, vomiting, etc. Wolpe emphasized that the patient should be well relaxed and he used hypnosis for this purpose. A so-called rational, a logically founded explanation, needs to be given to motivate the patient.

Example of rationale for relaxation and subsequent desensitization to drilling sound
Drilling sound has previously made you feel discomfort because you once experienced pain or discomfort when hearing it. However it is just a sound that you could learn to accept, when you know that it is not threatening any longer. If you relax, I can let you hear the drill from a distance while you remain relaxed, in order to practise not being affected by the sound. Are you ready fo this? Then we'll start with the relaxation. What is your level of tension on a scale 1-100, if 50 is supposed to be an average? Are you above or below 50?

Induction follows with suggestions of a really good feeling and deep relaxation. Hypnosis usually is the easiest way to teach patients to relax and stay relaxed while different stimuli are presented, until tolerated. Desensitization is started when the patient has relaxed to a level well under 50. A tension reduction of at least 20 units on the scale above can be expected after a short hypnotic induction. If this is enough you simply teach the art of holding on to the relaxation and the good feeling. Relaxation and successive approximation of fear provoking stimuli, at a rate adapted to the patient, are the most important factors for success.

An anxiety response can be triggered automatically by just the thought of dentistry and the threat still feels real. The fact that anxiety reflexes are learned through classical conditioning means that they can not be controlled by willpower. Patients sometimes feel ashamed about their lack of control until they get informed about the mechanisms at work. They often get very interested and highly motivated for treatment to overcome their problem.

If the induction of hypnosis makes the patient feel good and if the level of tension is 40 or lower desensitizing of the stimulus causing discomfort (drill noise in the example above) can be carried out. In dental care there is an unique opportunity to use real stimuli instead of imagined ones, which is the original. In vivo desensitization usually goes faster and is therefore generally preferred. The principle is to gradually approach what generates fear and anxiety. At the least sign of stress, a stop is made, relaxation is renewed and a step back on the list of graded stimuli is taken. Everything must not be done at once. The direction will always be forwards to progress, remembering the fact that anxiety and relaxation are incompatible.

Observing and taking into account patient reactions during ongoing dental treatment is important. Even if hypnosis has not been planned from the beginning it is usually recommendable to make an induction if signs of tension or discomfort are seen. The most common signs are sweat drops on the forehead or on the upper lip as well as muscular tension in the hands or face. Another indication for hypnos is when patients tell you about feeling discomfort or tension.

The few minutes you spend on promoting relaxation usually give good payoff. Many problems may arise if the tension is allowed to increase. The treatment goes easier once the patient has relaxed. Even for a dentist or hygienist who quite often uses hypnosis, it's easy to forget about it, if you happen to be focused on something else. The signs of tension, listed above, should be taken as absolute indications that hypnosis should be used directly or that the treatment should be interrupted and postponed.

5. Operant conditioning. Exposure

The word operant refers to the active choice of behavior. As with classical conditioning, the time factor is important in operant conditioning. If a behaviour is given an immediate reward or punishment it will be associated with the consequence. If this is punishment the behaviour usually will be avoidance. *A burnt child dreads the fire* is a saying that is a good description of avoidance due to operant conditioning. In order for such a child not to get caught in avoidance, playing with fire under controlled conditions is helpful. The principle of exposure is that irrational anxiety subsides automatically, if you stay in the disturbing situation long enough to realize that there will be no "punishment."

Dental treatment must not be seen as threatening, provided that the perceived risk is eliminated or under control. Avoidance is a behaviour that is learned by operant conditioning. Irrational fear can be maintained for decades by avoidance. If safety is guaranteed and the patient still feels uncomfortable it is obvious that the feeling has to do with earlier experiences in a similar environment or situation. If no immediate treatment is planned the anxiety of being in a fear provoking environment will subside automatically. In this case treatment consists of letting the patient be in the alarming environment until the fear is gone.

Let us suppose that the avoidance started after painful dental treatment. When a new treatment is to be performed, even if guaranteed to be painless, the old memories cause fear and the patient feels discomfort. Grabbing the armchair or tensing the face or hands is a common behaviour that maybe makes the patient feel prepared. The fact that the jaw and the teeth have become totally numb after chemical anesthesia does not free the patient from expecting pain. The reason is that the so called security behaviour tells the brain that pain is expected. Therefore the security behaviours must stop. Without these behaviours the patient will be exposed to the own feeling of anxiety. The result will be that the emotion subsides and then it will be possible to realize that there is no pain.

Along with desensitization, exposure is one of the most important principles for treatment of anxiety. It is said that the author Goethe cured his fear of heights by asking his friends to let him hang out of a tall church tower. They were told to tie him with safe ropes and not to free him until he had calmed down. He obviously trusted his friends and the ropes. He also understood that a feeling can't be at its maximum for more than a certain time especially if there is no real danger.

The two treatment methods; desensitization and exposure assume that the anxiety response is learned. Both methods are used for the purpose of learning and relearning. If a person realizes that the anxiety, logically seen, is excessive and therefore dares to expose himself/herself to it without doing anything else he will be cured. Anxiety gradually decreases and eventually disappears. All security behaviours must be removed. They only give a short and temporary reduction of anxiety, but delay or prevent cure. Anxiety reduction is perceived as a reward of the security behaviour. Therefore there is a risk that it may continue together with the false idéa that it has increased safety. There must be not even a twinkle of the eye.

Patients who can not relax deeply enough for desensitization are treated with exposure. They may feel discomfort just by sitting in a dental chair. The operator promises full control of everything that happens and ensures that there is no real need to be afraid. After a period of conversation with the patient sitting in the treatment room, discomfort has usually disappeared or decreased by itself. Another way of exposure is letting the patient look at well-chosen video films about dental treatment until they become accustomed to them. If some relaxation is also included in the treatment the effect will be maximized as it combines exposure with desensitization.

If sounds from the drill feel scary although it's known that no drilling will occur, the fear can be said to be irrational. One can get used to a sound if it is neutral without any special meaning. As long as there is no risk for any pain or anything else that possibly could be threatening the sound should cause no reactions, which is the goal of treatment. Exposure does not rely primarily on relaxation, but on the fact that the anxiety drops automatically after a period of exposure. This should preferably continue until the anxiety has totally declined.

The exposure is carried out under safe conditions. For those who have been afraid of dental care due to pain it is of course important to let them experience painless treatment. It requires some courage in those who choose to be exposed to treatment that has previously been causing pain, or in terms of CBT, been punished.

6. Cognitive behaviour therapy (CBT)

CBT is a psychotherapeutic treatment method aimed at changing harmful thoughts and behaviours, which are seen as learned. All measurable responses in the organism are usually regarded as behaviours and the triggers are called stimuli. In this book a separation between behaviours and reflexes is made. Radical behaviourists together with the founder, B.F. Skinner, has only been interested in measurable effects of stimuli. Psychological events they consider impossible to judge and therefore have given intrapsychic events the term "the black box".

With modern technique, measurements can be made in different parts of the brain. Changes there may be of interest in the same way as other measurable responses. Therefore, in CBT, which is largely based on the same theoretical fundament as behaviourism, it is now considered that cognitions also play an important role. Within physics, a clear distinction is made between will-controlled behaviours and reflexes. So-called automatic thoughts can be considered as cognitive reflexes. Will controlled thoughts, on the other hand, are a form of chosen behaviours that may be influenced by means of operant conditioning, i.e. by immediate reward or punishment.

New, realistic thoughts	*New behaviours*	*New kind of reward*
Fine needle	*Stay*	*Self confidence*
Anesthesia is good	*See what happens*	*Praise*
It doesn't hurt	*To relax*	*Hope of cure*

2 Thought reflexes
(Automatic neg.
thoughts)
It hurts
It,s harming
Torture

1 Stimulus	**3 Behaviour**	**4 Reward**
(Syringe)	Avoidance	Fear is reduced
	Tensing up	Feels prepared
	Escape	Fear disappears

2 Emotion and reflexes
Fear and physiological
reflexes (muscular ten-
sion, pulse, sweating,
etc.)

Time 0 ....**0,1 seconds**

Fig. 2 In people with needle phobia the sight of a syringe (1) simultaneously triggers reflexes of automatic thoughts (2) and an emotion of fear, combined with physiologic reflexes(2). The behaviour(3) that follows (to the right) is governed by an internal reward (4) consisting of reduction or elimination of fear. If alternative thoughts are thought immediately after the automatic ones, also alternative behaviours may be chosen, which leads to cure if continued. The easy way of instant anxiety reduction ends up in a vicious circle as the only reward comes from inside the organism. Health-promoting options are italicized above the upper line.

Reflexes are triggered within a fraction of a second when a syringe is seen. A typical reaction pattern in needle phobia is illustrated in the figure above. An automatic negative thought can't be abolished but it is possible to think another thought immediately after the automatic one. This needs to be trained. The model can be used to make the patient understand how remedy is possible. You explain how fear has been learned, and how a vicious circle is maintained by automatic negative thoughts and behaviours. It is important to learn new ways of thinking and to realize that relaxation is a better behaviour than consciously tensing. The best way of gaining control is obtained through open communication with an open minded operator.

Painless injection is possible and if it can be demonstrated, this is very valuable. With the right technique, it is easy, at least in the side regions of the upper jaw. Treatment rational (logical explanation) should be given. An example: *"Viewing a needle automatically triggers thoughts, feelings and reflexes, whether you want it or not. It recalls previous experiences of discomfort. This has nothing to do with today's reality. I think that you will realize that I can anesthetise so gently that you will find it painless. Even if avoidance or escape gives an immediate relief of fear, it does not solve the problem. To get a change you have to realize that my way of anesthetising is gentle and relaxing. You can abandon tightening your muscles. Otherwise you send a signal to the brain that you are still expecting pain."*

Reflexes and feelings cannot be directly influenced by willpower. They are a result of the thinking pattern, based on earlier experiences. One can choose to test new thoughts and behaviours according to Figure 2. To manage this it is necessary to be brave enough to rely on the operator and give it a try. The reward may be that the operator shows appreciation and that self-confidence is strengthened when progress is made. Patients can learn to analyze their own behaviour and to give themselves praise after each progress. Drilling noise is a stimulus which, like the syringe and the needle, can trigger discomfort and negative thoughts. Instead of following the old thinking pattern, new and realistic thoughts can be added. It should be done immediately. Therefore the new thought must be at hand. This makes it possible to test also a new behaviour, which gives the opportunity to discover how the discomfort is automatically reduced when the vicious circle has been broken.

One tip for self treatment may be that, if you feel scared ask yourself: What was the trigger? What stimulus (S) scared me? Focus on the feeling in order to make conscious which cognitions (thoughts, memories or images) come up? It could be assumed that it is something that reminds of dental treatment and the cognition may be: "it's painful." S is also the first letter of the word STOP, which reminds one to stay in the feeling and to ask what thoughts are associated with it. The letter **T** stands for **thought**. The first thought may be "pain". The letter **O** in STOP stands for **other thoughts** that might be more realistic. Example:" I can be calm! Painlessness has been promised, relaxation seems to work." **P** stands for **praise**. Give yourself praise every time you have managed to identify an automatic negative thought and to directly find a realistic thought. One should always praise and reward oneself for being flexible in thinking and behaving.

The first thought is not always realistic because the situation is not quite the same. A patient who has tried out alternative ways of thinking may have found some thoughts that are at least as credible as the automatic ones. To find alternatives is often eased if it is made together with a therapist who could be the dentist, the hygienist or a psychotherapist. The therapist makes a list of the patient's negative thoughts and after having found and disputed the credibility of the alternatives, training is started. As soon as the therapist tells one of the listed negative thoughts the patient should mention an alternative immediately. The training is preferably made under hypnosis.

7. What is hypnosis, suggestion and susceptibility?

A common labelling of hypnosis is an altered state of consciousness (ASC). In clinical hypnosis relaxation and calmness are important ingredients. If emphasis is on these, hypnosis and relaxation can be regarded as almost identical states. A deeply relaxed patient feels no anxiety, no pain and has not exaggerated quenching reflex. Secretion of saliva and tendency to bleed are also hampered. Helping patients to relax takes only a few minutes after having got their permission. It starts with restraining the inflow of sensory stimuli.

What happens if you ask a patient to close the eyes? Evident is, that visual impressions disappear and external stimuli will be perceived mainly through hearing and, if a hand is laid upon the shoulder, through the sense of feeling. A restriction of incoming stimuli automatically takes place when attention is focused on listening or trying to understand the meaning of something heard or felt.

The result will be a trance state usually of short duration, if it is not maintained or deepened by well-timed suggestions. As the voice of the caregiver is the main channel of incoming stimuli, it can be used to arrest attention and then to promote relaxation and calm feelings by means of positive words and a calm tone and rhythm. Limited and focused attention increases suggestibility. This means that feelings and cognitions, evoked in the subject by the operator, will have a strong influence. Every word should be chosen carefully in order to create a maximum of calmness and wellbeing.

If there is tension in some part of the body after eye closure, attention is primarily directed towards this. It is much easier to direct attention to an existing sensation than to an idea of something else. After a while, tiredness will automatically evoke feelings of heaviness, and that is the right moment for suggestions of relaxation and heaviness. Sensations of heaviness and warmth will soon dominate and the patient will tend to linger in them. This can be seen as a sign of hypnosis if the attention lingers spontaneously for 10 seconds or more.

The reason to stay in hypnosis usually is that it feels good and pleasant to experience relaxation and calm feelings. Such feelings are important for mental stability and health in adults as well as in babies. According to Braid, focus lingering on one single feeling or idea is typical for some initial stages of hypnosis, which made him suggest the term monoideism. The hypnotic state means being in the own inner world, to be passive and oriented to experiencing what spontaneously attracts attention. That means, not making any conscious choices of thoughts or behaviours. The same apply to meditation techniques.

The main stream of stimuli comes via the operators voice. Monotony and physical inactivity lead to inactivation of the patient's brain cortex. Hypnosis involves selective thinking, which means partial inactivation of the brain cortex. This can be triggered as a conditioned response or it can be the result of an emotional state with activation of the parasympathetic nerve system. It causes inactivation of consciously controlled activities, as analytical thinking and muscular activities. Attention then tend to linger on spontaneous physical sensations or on relaxing mental images and memories.

Working with hypnosis involves observation of reflexes, in order to make the subject aware of them. Your understanding of what is behind them facilitates the formulation of suggestions, because reflexes have connection with and depend on where the spontaneous attention is at the very moment. By knowing this you can strengthen focus, when it is on something that is calming and relaxing, such as calm breathing, slow breathing, and immobility. Use monotonous repeating of selected stimuli like words about body sensations of heaviness, warmth or relaxing mental images or memories. The main aim is to trigger a calm, positive emotion and a relaxation reflex. Passiveness and lack of initiative should be promoted and fortified. Mental images can be used as distraction and sometimes may lead to complete dissociation.

Physical blocking of outer stimuli can be used, but unwanted stimuli can be also be blocked by focusing of attention. Those parts of the brain that are involved in reality testing will then be inactivated. The regulation is made in the reticular activating system (RAS), situated at the core of the brain stem. This is the center of attention in the brain and it acts as a filter that lets only important stimuli pass, thus influencing the information we receive. That is the cause of selective perception and thinking, typical for hypnosis. Lack of outer stimuli automatically increases focus on the few remaining stimuli. These are the voice of the operator, body sensations and automatic movements and reflexes in the form of mental images, cognitions and feelings. The similarity between hypnosis and meditation states is apparent.

Alertness varies during night and day in periods of 90 minutes (ultradian rhythm). When it is low, a tired person, trying to solve problems by logic reasoning, but not allowing himself to take pauses, can be seen sitting quite immobile with an absent gaze in a spontaneous trance. Even if he or she believes that they are working hard, thinking has made a halt and the whole organism is at rest. The attention is absorbed by the dominating feeling of tiredness. Unfortunately there is a lot of people who get burned out because they don't pay attention to signals of tiredness. They do not want to slow down and therefore try to suppress all feelings of tiredness.

Miracles can come from learning to welcome impulses to rest and to take a pause and reserve some time for relaxation.

If induction of hypnosis is started when the degree of alertness is high the subject's need for relaxation may be limited and perhaps there will be a need for activity. As major physical activity is out of question during treatment only mental activity can be offered. To start this is easy and when it has begun it will continue automatically as long as the need exists. Material will come from the inner world of imaginations (global awareness) where our memories, imaginations and thoughts are stored.

In an altered state of consciousness (ASC), logic thinking and reality testing of sensory stimuli as well as of mental images have been replaced by emotionally guided awareness, directed to inner experiences. Therefore hypnosis can be regarded as an attention psychology. In the everyday waking state we expect the awareness to be consciously and voluntarily guided but sometimes it gets captured and turned inwards by spontaneous reflexes in the form of bodily sensations or by mental images, notions or memories.

If nothing in the environment catches the attention it will spontaneously go inwards, usually to the experience of relaxation and calmness. Monotony can achieve this. ASC then becomes a passive state, free from consciously guided initiatives. The awareness is restricted to experiencing and feeling the own inner world. The position of the body is not altered, nothing is questioned or criticized and the willingness to cooperate is heightened. Behaviours are replaced by reflexes triggered by the mental images that stay in focus. They can be elicited as associations, expectations, or by the use of conscious suggestion.

Conscious and willful effort to guide the attention does not happen in hypnotized people. They are in a passive state without logical or analytical thinking. Therefore the induction may consist of different ways to tire activities demanding effort. The operator promotes passiveness in the subject and puts focus on bodily reflexes such as relaxation, catalepsy, anesthesia, and automatic, muscular movements. Focus on these is called local awareness. It can effortlessly shift to the experience of cognitions (global awareness) and focus on visual, sensual, auditory olfactory or taste sensations like in a dream. Only a very small part of the material, stored in the brain can reach consciousness at a given moment and become available for experiencing.

Spontaneity means that emotion is engaged. If the whole attention is directed to bodily sensations one of these will soon be perceived stronger than the others. A common experience is relaxation combined with a sensation of extreme heaviness in the parts of the body that are well supported. Another sensation is immobility and rigidity that helps the body keep its position focused and engaged.

Unconsciously guided retaining of a given position is called catalepsy. This often happens spontaneously when attention is focused and engaged. The word catalepsy is sometimes described as a waxy flexibility of the joints. This phenomenon is caused by the fact that only so much muscular energy, necessary to retain a given position, is activated. If a cataleptic arm is given a new position it will remain in the new position due to the fact that no initiatives are taken by the hypnotized subject. Another form of catalepsy is when a well supported body part is relaxed and therefore does not change position.

Sometimes unpleasant memories or imaginations are triggered spontaneously. This leads to a negative ASC with focus on threatening phantasies. In a clinical setting it is a challenge to help the patient come out of a negative state of consciousness. Calming information, founded on the operators true willingness to help and to tell facts that make the patient rely on you and feel safe are crucial. The willingness to cooperate is thus strengthened. Threatening phantasies are disputed and a positive ASC, including relaxation can then be induced.

Relaxation usually feels good and the pleasure is strengthened if associations to positive memories and imaginations are evoked. This is facilitated if these topics have been mentioned already at the preliminary talk, before the hypnosis induction. The patient may be informed that relaxation is recommendable and that it opens the possibility to indulge in positive imagery like for instance hobby activities, pleasurable memories, nature scenery or anything they prefer.

Positive words like pleasant, comfortable, enjoyable etc. will strengthen a good feeling. A factor of great importance to motivate a patient to stay in hypnosis is the operators talents in creating lust for cooperation and a feeling of security. A safe and friendly behaviour will contribute to this. Clear, well formulated instructions focusing on deep relaxation usually works. However, the operator must exercise in order to gain security, approximately in the same way as actors or a lecturers need to prepare themselves.

Spontaneous ASC is an everyday phenomena, often in connection with experiences generating emotions. The trigger may be reunions, catching films, or practising hobby activities, creating a feeling of flow. That is a pleasant ASC of complete concentration and having full control over an ongoing activity. When feeling engaged in a film, this may be felt like being in the center of the events and being in the place where everything is unfolded. Role playing and other forms of activity, which requires feeling and engagement are often done in a state of trance, i.e. hypnosis (ASC). A simple definition of ASC, trance and hypnosis is "an emotional state, when spontaneous attention, without effort ingers on one isolated experience for at least ten seconds." Braid called it monoideism.

Every person continuously creates conceptions of our world. From every word in the language associations are made. Using experiences, even if they are sometimes very limited, paradigms are created and from these are made presuppositions in order to make the world predictable. Naturally mistakes can be made or things may have changed over time making the observations that lead to certain presumptions outdated. Nevertheless they were the best interpretations that could be made at the time and will be used as guidelines until new experiences lead to new, hopefully realistic presumptions.

In hypnosis it is possible to influence false and harmful thought- and behaviour patterns in an effective way. These patterns are stored in the unconscious and from there they influence both perception and thinking. The human brain is working in two different ways, consciously and unconsciously. The hypnotic state sometimes can be characterized as deep relaxation and rest, and sometimes there is a dreamlike mental activity, accompanied by associations to unconscious stored material, such as, for instance, certain thinking patterns.

By presenting to a person in hypnosis different examples of alternative interpreting facts these can be seen in a new light. Metaphors and story-telling may be used.

Perception as well as conscious, critical awareness that ought to be related to reality can be dominated by old thinking patterns, ideas and memories, retrieved from the unconscious mind. The whole organism can be guided by unconscious influence in the hypnotic state but also in the waking state, like for example in people with phobias and people with fixed ideas. In hypnosis it is always the own ideas and imaginations that influence and guide the responses, but the idéas can be triggered by someone else. Of course there are limits to how much a person is willing to let somebody else evoke unconsciously triggered reflexes but that will be no problem if an agreement is made from the beginning on what type of suggestions may be given. As a guarantee against unwanted influence, it may be settled in advance with the subject that he is encouraged to interrupt the trance at any time if feeling uncomfortable or hesitant about it. Kay Thompson found resemblance between deep hypnosis and the REM-stage of sleep.

People with nightmares may benefit from instructions and suggestions of how to handle unwanted dreams.

If a subject is asked to direct the gaze steadily to a certain point, this can be done by conscious willpower but the spontaneous attention does not always follow where the eyes go. If you put your hand on the subject's shoulder you can be sure that this will attract the attention. When using hypnosis it is important to keep track of where the attention is for the moment and to make the subject aware of involuntary reflexes. In classic hypnosis according to Braid the focus is guided to the blink reflex. Suggestions of heaviness in the eyelids are aimed at eye closure and "sleep". In clinical hypnosis the suggestions nowadays are aimed at deep relaxation.

Children are emotional creatures with good phantasy and therefore they are very susceptible to hypnosis. However the susceptibility to word-based hypnosis is limited before six years of age. The greatest susceptibility is considered to be in the age of 7-14 years and then it slowly declines. The famous Swedish hypnotherapist Poul Bjerre (1876- 1964) meant that it would be a good idea to preserve the suggestibility by training. Today many people utilize meditation, which like hypnosis lead to activation of the parasympathetic nerve system, involving calm and relaxation. Bjerre's idea, that training already from early age is recommendable, seems plausible.

The susceptibility to hypnosis is varying and has to do with suggestibility. This is an inborn quality, highly associated with how prone attention is to linger on a single sensation or imagination. Emotions increase this tendency. In this context, ten seconds is a long time, indicating a hypnotic state. People knowing that they are suggestible should be careful before taking important decisions. It is recommendable that they sleep on it, to enable balanced and realistic assessment instead of being guided by emotions and suggestions.

Suggestibility and being inclined to enter hypnosis gives access to phantasy and emotion. Artists usually are susceptible to suggestion. Like other human qualities the degree of suggestibility is different. It can be measured with tests. There are similarities between the concepts of motivation and suggestion. Coué at the time proceeded from the concept of suggestion and made clear the mechanisms at work. (Chapter 8).

The concept of motivation means a psychological drive for action. The word can be used as a substitute for words like need, wish, inspiration and lust etc. A motive consists of two components working together, emotion and a goal in the form of an image. The emotion may either exist before the goal is set or it could be the result of focusing on an imagination that evokes a need (emotion) and then the emotion together with the imagined goal becomes a motive.

A thirsty person will look for something to drink and a person that is not so thirsty can be made feel thirst if a drink is presented together with scenes that awaken positive associations, memories of thirst and good feelings when drinking. The willingness to cooperate is an important motive in hypnosis. In self hypnosis the calm and pleasant feeling from relaxation may be motivating as well as memories of a safe place, or happy moments.

8. Direct och indirect suggestion. Motivation to relax

The whole idea about suggestion is built on the fact that human beings have an inner, imaginary world with representations of the outer world, a kind of model of this. The conscious mind has only place for a very small part of what is stored in the brain. Things that are important in everyday life can, however, easily be made conscious. Some material may be less available, and some will remain unconscious. You may have totally forgotten things that you once learned, but sometimes you instinctively know that there is something unavailable deep in your memory. The more you try to remember the more impossible it seems to be, but when you stop straining, it happens that a memory comes up spontaneously. The unconscious mind has then been working with associations until a memory could be presented. It is important to know that the memory that comes up in the conscious mind is a construct that must not necessarily represent the truth.

In the ordinary state of consciousness with mainly outgoing attention the majority of the incoming stimuli are weeded in the prolonged medulla. Only the ones that pass through the filter will be consciously recognised. Emotions are evoked and reality testing takes place. For example an elongated subject can evoke a spontaneous image of a snake. Reality testing can end up in replacing the first image with a reality rooted image of a branch. When reality testing does not take place, like in hypnosis, the first image may be reinforced by emotions and end up in a hallucination in highly suggestible people.

To give a suggestion maximal effect the mind needs to be prepared in advance. In the exemple above the preparation was perhaps the information that the region was rich of dangerous snakes. Worry about how difficult it can be to detect them and how easily it could happen that you tread on one augments the vigilance. That activates unconsciously stored images of snakes and these work as indirect suggestions.

In clinical settings there is often a need for suggestions to reduce fear and to arouse calmness. This can be accomplished by talking about things that engage the patient's positive feelings, either by reassuring comments concerning the treatment or by distracting with talk about topics from the patient's sphere of interests. This is usually revealed rather early in a conversation and the clever operator should listen carefully to what the patient mentions.

A clinician should be seriously interest in his patients, be calm but also show an optimistic attitude. What can be perceived as boasting in other circumstances may help the patient to feel safe. To inform about the own rich experience may sometimes influence the patient to rely on you. Also tell that you always look for signs of discomfort and that you will stop working immediately, if you see any.

Formulation of suggestions should aim at eliciting goal images and keep them in focus. Direct suggestion should be clear and pronounced in a secure way that doesn't give room for any doubt. The person giving suggestions should express them so that she/he believes in the own words. If a subject is in deep trance direct suggestion normally will gain effect, i.e. be realized. The art of giving suggestions, pared with experience, good observation skills and a sense of timing will help to maximize the effect of given suggestions and to assess the result. It is recommendable to draw attention to this to show that other forces than will power are at work.

Indirect suggestion means to evoke imaginations and to prepare the psyche for some sort of reflexive behaviour, without giving specific suggestions or commands. The idea is to catch attention, but also to let the subject be free to choose among several given options. If the goal is anesthesia the idea of being free from pain may be presented by telling examples of people getting wounded without feeling or noticing it, because their attention was completely focused on something else. After that the subject could be inspired to mentally leave the body and go to some pleasant place and stay there as long as wanted. A final suggestion could be." When you are there your index finger will lift and stay up as a sign to me that everything is OK with you."

Indirect suggestion can be used to prepare for good emotions by using interspersed, positive words of different forms like *comfort, happy, nice, relaxing, enjoy, good, free, calm, fine, safe,* etc. By choosing positive conversational topics from the patient's point of view, a good feeling during hypnosis is eased. Suitable topics may be hobbies, holidays, own children or other important persons, animals, natural scenery etc. The general idea is to make the patient's spontaneous imaginations be the focal point.

The great advantage of indirect suggestion is that it does not create resistance, since it is not insistent. Of course the acceptance of a suggestion will be easier if there exists a corresponding need to satisfy. Patients with fear have a need for safety, sympathy and understanding. If such suggestions are given they have good possibilities to be accepted and realized. After that the land is well prepared also for more suggestions.

A direct suggestion to go to a restaurant can be rejected even by a person with a certain hunger, if there is something that feels more important at the moment. Hunger feelings can be strengthened by indirect suggestions in the form of pleasant smells or tempting pictures of food. When this kind of cues work as indirect suggestions and precede a direct suggestion of going to the restaurant the probability for acceptance of this suggestion is increased.

Certain motives that have been formed at early age under influence of strong emotion may cause certain thought patterns and presuppositions. From these life rules can be formed, which build on how life events are interpreted in the light of the presuppositions. If a life rule is to always be in control and never rely on somebody else, an induction of hypnosis will be difficult or impossible. If you manage to convince the subject that hypnosis is always self suggestion and that it means more self control, this may be crucial for a change of attitude to hypnosis.

According to Maslow's theory about our basic needs and their strength, the need to protect oneself from physical damage belongs to the strongest. He calls them organical needs. It is understandable that a patient who actively maintains an idea of risk for damage will not feel safe and therefore has difficulties to relax. The need to feel safe belongs to the emotional motives and is also very strong. An empathetic, calm, friendly and secure attitude in the operator and his team can meet this need.

Once a patient feel safe with a therapist the social motives tend to be activated. They deal with the need for social relatedness or love, belongingness, sympathy and common values and beliefs. Social motives are thought to be the most important in making religious societies stay together. In psychotherapy it has been shown that it is crucial for the results that patient and therapist like each other. The same is also true for teacher-pupil relations. Popular teachers have been shown to get better results of their teaching.

Human beings are social creatures which means, for better or worse, that the acceptance of suggestions from a leader is facilitated, and so is the willingness to cooperate with a hypnotist, as soon as the hypnotist's role as a leader is accepted together with the own role as a subject. It is an instinct to follow leaders, especially if they have high prestige or have a role that evokes expectations of leadership. The willingness to uncritically obey to and cooperate with an authority or a hypnotist may be a strong motivator. Therefore people with high status in a society have a great responsibility. You could just think of the famous experiment of Milgram about obedience, where a person with the title professor made the participants make horrible things. They could not know that the suffering that they were ordered to administer to the participants in an experimental group was not real. Therefore it is astonishing that only a few refused to obey.

Emotion usually guides behaviour to a much higher degree than rationality, based on facts and informed decision. The need for good relationships may be stronger than the need to struggle against disregarding of obvious facts. To be accepted by a group you must stand up for common ideas and values due to the need for harmonic relations. If somebody is critical, this leads to a conflict of motives, creating a cognitive dissonance with bad feelings (Festinger) and disharmony. This will continue until a resolution of the conflict is found.

In order to increase the chance for a certain suggestion to be accepted the tactic built on limitation of choices could be used. The subject is forced to choose among only a few alternatives. Either of them implicates that it will end up in a certain result. Example: "Do you want to shut down the computer now or in 15 minutes"? In the case that two alternatives are given but, both of them mean going into trance this is called double bind. Example: " Do you prefer to go in trance slowly or rapidly"?

To suggest means in everyday speech to propose something. The proposal is directed both to the conscious and the unconscious mind. If the suggestion is repeated in a monotonous way the conscious mind gets tired but unconscious activity will start automatically. The attention field becomes narrowed and associations emanating from the suggestion start. They will evoke emotion and contribute to making a clear image of what is suggested. However it isn't always the same image that pops up i different people as a result of a suggestion. (Fig. 3) When the emotions support the imaginated change this will be accepted as a goal. Then it has become a working suggestion, a psychological drive to realize the suggestion.

Cartoon by Allan Perolainen

Fig. 3 Suggestions may evoke different imaginations in different people.

9. Susceptibility to suggestion and hypnotic capacity

In older literature the depth of hypnosis is often divided into three stages, light, medium and deep. This type of division is founded mainly on reactions to a common test of suggestibility. Hypnotic capacity is regarded to be related to the degree of susceptibility, assessed in a suggestibility test.

Dave Elman has his own view based on his clinical experience, and he is critical to the commonly used scales. He means that physical relaxation in combination with mental relaxation that characterizes a somnambulistic, deep state of hypnosis can reached by a majority of people. A few people go direct into a deep hypnosis but many more can go deep, if they go into a light stage at first, characterized by physical relaxation. Then they can go deep by mental relaxation. He also describes other, even deeper hypnotic states of which the "Elman state" is of special interest when it is about hypnotic anesthesia.

For a clinician it is important to know what type of suggestion that will work in every single case. Even if a subject after a standard test, is considered to be low susceptible, suggestions of relaxation, calmness, heaviness and warmth may be effective in a clinical situation. Suggestions of numbness and total freedom from pain should not be used in these cases because they will probably fail. Instead the possibility to disregard pain to a certain degree may have a good chance to be accepted. Also distraction by focusing on positive memories like in day- dreaming may work.

On an average the susceptibility to hypnosis in a population is divisible into the following categories.
Unsusceptible   10 %
Light trance   35 %
Medium trance 35 %
Deep trance   20 %

Out of the 10 % of subjects counted as unsusceptible most of them will, under favourable circumstances, go into trance. Below are examples of criterias often used as indicators of depth of trance.

Light stage: Heaviness of limbs. Suggestions of lokal feeling of warmth may be effective. Suggestions of limb and eyelid catalepsy work. Ideomotor activity.

Medium stage: Only the voice ot the operator is heard. Complete catalepsy of limbs. Glove anesthesia. Feels the difference between trance state and ordinary consciousness. Manages to stand drilling of tooth and depuration without anaesthesia.

Deep stage: Fixed gaze when eyes are open. Can open eyes without affecting trance state. Suggestions of amnesia are often effective and in the deepest stage amnesia may be spontaneous. Posthypnotic amnesia. Retarded, slow movements if conscious movement is requested. Age regression. Positive och negative visual- and auditory hallucinations. Every kind of post-hypnotic suggestions are possible. Tooth extractions can be made without anesthesia.

For a clinician the division into the groups above may help to some degree, but there are seldom strict boundaries between the different stages. Sometimes it it obvious that subjects in light trance can be made rather independent of chemical analgesia. Sometimes people in the medium stage may be so focused on pain that they insist on getting an injection.

The majority of people has the ability to go into a trance state and to benefit from this. It is recommendable that the operator for future sessions makes a note about the suggestibility (0-3) and what type of suggestions that have worked well.

10. Hypnosis, emotion och spontaneous attention

Hypnosis is an emotional state with attention mainly directed inwards. It can also be seen as a regressive state (going back to earlier developmental stages) when subjects, like infants are emotionally guided. Babies are emotional creatures without any ability for abstract thinking. Emotions of calmness and safety alternate with anxiety or exaltation. For a sound development the baby requires some help to regulate the emotions so that they don't get too strong and so that they shift at a suitable rate. A child needs somebody who can help with these things. The way of doing this has similarities to an induction of hypnosis. There is a saying that mothers are the best hypnotists of the world, which means that they are skilled at getting their babies calm. Thumb sucking has been seen as self hypnosis.

Your own positive mindset will immediately affect the tone of your voice and body language, putting your subject at ease. When you're warm, open, friendly, smiling and welcoming, the other person has no choice but to feel that as well. This, coupled with the fact that only 7% of communication is verbal and the other 93% is extra-verbal makes it obvious that you must have a positive mind-set to be a good hypnotist. What you communicate by tone of voice and body language is so much influenced by your unconscious mind that you can't fake it.

The autonomic nerve system consists of two parts, the sympathetic and the parasympathetic nerve system working in an antagonistic way. When the sympathetic system is activated the adrenal glands produce adrenalin and noradrenalin. The hormones go to the bloodstream and cause emotional and muscular tension. The original function is to make the body prepared for fight or flight.

The parasympathetic system works by producing acetylcholine in the nerve synapses, which results in calm feelings and relaxation. Blood goes from the muscles to the inner organs and to the widened small capillaries in the hands. The hands become warm and the heart rate becomes slow, typical parasympathetic responses. If nothing in the environment is threatening or disturbing, the autonomic system may go to rest. That is not hypnosis because trance means emotionalization, which means activity in both the sympathetic and in the parasympathetic nerve systems.

In hypnosis mainly the parasympathetic system is dominating but the sympathetic system is prepared to work antagonistically if anything upsets. By inducing a shift of attention from calming stimuli to more agitating, the attention can become more focused. An example of this is how an emotional atmosphere can be created when telling a ghost story. In the beginning the storyteller uses a calm tone of voice to make the listener feel safe and relaxed. This feeling is only counteracted by the fact that something scary is expected in a ghost story.

By telling a surprise and, at the same time altering the vocal pitch and volume, the storyteller activates the listener's sympathetic nerve system. As soon as the voice returns to normal and maybe becomes slow and soothing a shift to calmness occurs. Then the voice may suddenly get tense and agitated when telling some interesting observation and, influenced by this, sympathetic activation occurs, making the listener's attention even more focused. Usually the story ends with an explanation or some other fact that makes feelings calm down. Focus shifts to reality and a broader range of stimuli from the surroundings takes place. It's like going out of a trance.

When attention is focused on one task, all other activities demanding concentration are blocked. The initiative to take a decision to alter something that is out of focus is lacking. This is the reason for catalepsy, the tendency to keep the position that the body has, or has been given. The typical catalepsy is seen when some muscular tension is necessary for maintaining a body position. A relaxed subject doesn't move and a subject who is put in a position that calls for muscular tension will automatically release just as much tension as is needed to keep the position. When limbs are put i new positions they give the impression of a waxy flexibility. To evoke and demonstrate catalepsy is often a good way to induce hypnosis. It can be done without saying a word by changing position of the subject's limbs.

During dental treatment the patient is expected to sit or lie still with mouth open and moreover to be passive. Often he/she feels some tension but is nevertheless expecting to get and to follow directives. This means motivational factors good for hypnosis. After having the patient consciously focus attention, spontaneous feelings and body sensations of heaviness and relaxation may be chosen as the next focusing point. At the same time images from the patient's mental world can be triggered by suggestions if there is a need for activity of some sort. This must be mental since other activities are impossible in the situation. Mental images are, like emotions, spontaneous and autonomous reflexes.

Of all stimuli someone is exposed to only a few will be noted, as mentioned before. A weeding takes place in the reticular activating system, RAS, in the prolonged medulla. The primary aim of using hypnosis in dental – and medical praxis is to achieve calmness and relaxation , i.e. a parasympathetic response. Thanks to the patient's needs, hypnosis induction is facilitated when calming, monotonous verbal or tactile stimuli are used. In locked positions there is also an inborn reflex to react with a sudden parasympathetic relaxation response. This reminds of the reflex to play dead seen in some animals when threat and stress becomes too high and escape is impossible. (Benson)

Stomach breathing and slow pulse are signs of parasympathetic activity. In a very deep relaxation the lips are pale and no changes of body position are made. The pain threshold is high and the gagging reflex is weak. Attention lingers a long time on every perceived physical or mental experience, and it takes a long time to do something that calls for conscious effort. The decision taking and analytical functions are at rest, and the body is relaxed and passive.

The tendency to linger in an experience differs in different individuals already from birth and it is crucial for the susceptibility to hypnosis. Other factors are the actual emotional engagement, absence of disturbing impressions, the capability and motivation for taking a passive role and accept to be influenced by suggestions from somebody else or by self suggestions. No matter what, suggestion is only effective after being accepted and then it works as self suggestion whereby influence comes from the image derived from the own inner world. Being able to inspire lust for cooperation is important when hypnotizing.

Even if hypnosis has to do with inner experiences the communication between the hypnotist and the subject is always important. Already the first contact influences so that positive or negative expectations are generated. A goal should be to raise positive expectations and thoughts of being in safe hands. If the first contact with a clinic happens to be a nurse or a receptionist they should know how to convey this message.

When making an induction it is good if the level of stress in the patient is not too high, as it takes about 20 minutes for stress hormones in the blood to break down. When the stress level is only moderately elevated it can be balanced by the calm feelings that an induction of hypnosis produce. As fearful, tense and insecure patients feel a need for contact and support their emotional state may facilitate the induction under the condition that the operator is perceived as calm, secure an sympathetic.

Many patients are in a negative mood with unconscious focus on threatening images and memories. In the dental chair, they feel the demand to sit or lie still and to force themselves to open the mouth in spite of conflicting feelings. Their need for support makes them very susceptible to relaxing, calming suggestions. Some few promises, that everything will be done to make the patient feel safe may reduce the impact of threatening images. Thereafter focus may be directed to the remaining tensions and after a few moments to a beginning sense of relaxation. Suggestions of heaviness and calmness and relaxation will have a tremendous effect. Many patients need no further suggestions of relaxation. Distraction from the treatment can be offered. As an example can be mentioned a positive place or a pleasant memory.

11. Relaxation instruction for group or individuals

The relaxation instructions below are well suited as an introduction to hypnosis They may be used as a convincing example to let sceptics feel that there is no reason to refrain being influenced by relaxing suggestions individually or in a group setting. The subject(s) should be seated in an ordinary chair.

Instructions to a group
I will show you how easy it is to become relaxed, in only a couple of minutes. You should go from tension to relaxation. Put the hands on your thighs with palms turned upwards. There will be a certain tension in your arms. Keep them so until I tell you to turn them like this (show). Now lift your toes and feel the tension in your legs. Direct your gaze to a point in the ceiling and follow my instructions carefully.

- *Take a deep breath and hold it! Feel the tension in the abdomen and breast!*
- *Exhale and close your eyes! Relax your face!*
- *Inhale! Hold! When you exhale, let your head tilt forwards. Now! Relax!*
- *Inhale! Turn the hands when exhaling! Now! Hands and arms relax!*
- *Inhale! Hold the air, hold it. -Let go and relax your belly and your back!*
- *Inhale! Now, put your feet down and relax your legs. (Puff out loudly)*

- *Take a very deep breath! Hold it, hold it and let go, relaxing from head to toe. – Psch! Allow yourself to enjoy a deep relaxation! Just let yourself go! The breathing may continue at its own pace. You mustn't do anything. Feel the pleasure of becoming deeply relaxed!*

If the relaxation should be considered to be a hypnotic state depends above all on if there is a tendency to linger on an experience and, related to that, how strong the emotion is. When giving instructions to a group it can be observed that some people react stronger than others. This has often to do with an inborn susceptibility. To lead the exercise above is an educational experience that can be practised with a group or individually. Everything should be memorized so that instructions can be given without hesitation and in a suggestive way.

A caregiver who doesn't want to make a formal hypnotic induction is anyhow wise if he/she tries to give the patient a positive experience by stimulating calm and relaxed feelings. After some calming information it could be suggested that it might be more comfortable to have the eyes closed. Of course patients should be allowed to choose themselves, but they could at least be encouraged to try. Avoid to treat patients if you see that they tighten their muscles! Inspire them to relax!

Hypnosis has been described as a psychology of attention and as an emotional state. It can be triggered very quickly as a reflex, learned by conditioning. A dental patient, who has been hypnotized before and senses that it is time to relax will often do it spontaneously. This means that cognitive and physiologic responses have been triggered by stimuli that have bypassed the critical sense. The emotion aroused will accomplish that the attention lingers on responses that feels good and that the patient has experienced before.

A method for attracting the patients attention, emotions and unconscious mind is to use so called pacing which to begin with means adapting the own rhythm of breathing to the subject's. You should also strive to make a general adaptation to the patient's emotional state by talking slowlier when you see increasing relaxation. You should comment on the reflexes that you observe, i.e. the breathing, by repeating "breathing in – and out-"at the same pace as the subject is breathing. You will then create the same emotional state in yourself as you try to evoke in the patient, which means that you go into trance together with the subject without losing your role as the leader.

Pacing generates monotony and at the same time it prevents conscious activity. When the operator becomes more and more relaxed it can be heard on his/her voice and that will have a strong influence. Everything that is said should be built on true observations. This creates a positive attitude in the subject, a yes set with a tendency to accept what is said. Therefore it opens up for the acceptance of leading suggestions. When the subject has begun to relax it may be the right time for leading them into deep abdominal breathing.

12. Suggestibility tests

There are a great number of tests to assess suggestibility. They measure the ideomotor and ideosensory effects, and sometimes also register posthypnotic amnesia (memory loss). Positive tests are an effect of dissociation, which means that different processes in the brain can go on separately, without having any connections (associations) between them. Dissociation can occur between the conscious experience of a positive test and, at the moment unconscious memory of when suggestions were given and accepted. That memory is unconscious, i.e., dissociated from the experience of the ideomotor or ideosensory effect. Dissociation is the opposite to association.

Below are some useful tests, arranged with the 'easiest' first and the following ones with rising 'difficulty'. Every test builds on directing attention, first on possible changes that can happen without conscious effort and then to the experience of them, when they become realized. The aim is to create dissociation, in order to make the subject accept being guided by suggestions causing spontaneous, not well-controlled reflexes. Many subjects become fascinated when noticing, i.e. automatic movements like a finger or an arm lifting "by it self". A test works like a mini-trance

Every positive test increases the probability for a positive result of the following test. Therefore it may be wise to make the tests in the order presented below, beginning with those that statistically have the greatest chance to work. They are not primarily used to test suggestibility. The usual purpose is to make a person's attention shift from being directed outwards to being turned inwards to the astonishing effects of suggestion. The tests presented here are well proved and they provide an effective way of accomplishing this shift by letting the subjects perceive physiological changes as well as spontaneous mental images. Before using tests you should learn them by heart. It is recommended that you use a sound recorder in order to hear your own voice to decide if you sound convincing.

Arm catalepsy, arm lowering and arm heaviness
Start by asking for the patient's consent to a test of his ability to relax.

Please close your eyes! Lift the patient's hand a little and hold it there until it can be released without sinking. (if sinking just give suggestions of heaviness). If it's staying *continue:* **Your hand is light and floating. After a while, it will begin to relax and then it will feel heavier. You can let it sink down and at the same time feel how your whole body relaxes. The deepest relaxation you won't feel until the arm and hand have sunk all the way down to the armchair.**

Arm catalepsy and heavy arm
When I stroke your arm you can feel how it relaxes (Stroke). It will feel heavier and heavier until it feels as one with the armchair, pressing down all the time. (Stroke) Heavy! It is heavy as metal, iron or lead! It is as one with the armchair! (Stroke) Unmovable! It is as glued to the armchair. Extremely heavy! Can't be lifted. (This is only said if there are signs indicating immobility) It's a good feeling isn't it? Patient nodding – **Good! Take a deep breath and notice the relaxation spreading through the whole body!**

Comments: The phrase:"isn't it" is meant to be perceived, not as a question but rather as an established finding. Of course you can challenge the subject by asking him to try to lift the arm, but then immediately add: *"it is impossible. The more you try the heavier it feels. It's pressing downwards"* That is the ultimate challenge to give. If you use it, you should be quite sure that the suggestion will work. This is very probable in cases where the arm is comfortably resting and relaxation is obvious. As hypnosis means reluctance to take any initiatives there is not much motivation to follow a suggestion involving conscious effort. The subject is more motivated to follow suggestions of heaviness, immobility as well as the suggestion that it is impossible to lift the arm. Such a suggestion causes a little confusion and should be followed by encouragement to continue to enjoy relaxation.

Arm catalepsy and arm rigidity

Raise the subject's arm in an upright position and give non verbal suggestions that it should remain there by embracing the arm near the shoulder with both your hands and slide them upwards two or three times. At the same time give verbal suggestions of stiffness. *I am holding your arm in an upright position. It is straight and becomes more and more rigid. It is straight and stiff. Now imagine a metal bar inside the arm keeping it straight. Straight, rigid and impossible to bend. Straight and rigid. Straight and rigid. Impossible to bend. Completely straight and rigid as a steel bar.*

Comments: when an arm is lifted up by the operator and stretched in an upright position it usually will remain in this position (catalepsy) or, in a few cases. it starts to sink down as it feels heavy. If this happens go directly to suggestions of increasing heaviness. Never give any verbal suggestions until you have assessed the effect of the non verbal ones. Use verbal suggestions only as a complement and they will never fail.

Eyelid catalepsy

With the eyelids comfortably closed you can look up to your forehead and imagine a green spot in the middle of it. Keep the eyes closed and relax all the small muscles around them. As you do so imagine the green

spot here! (put a finger at a point in the center of the forehead) When you can see the green you can feel, at the same time the eyelids relaxing, so that they feel comfortably and firmly closed. All the tiny muscles around them become so relaxed that they will be inactivated. The eyelids are comfortably and firmly closed. They are completely relaxed and so tight together that they feel like glued. Just focus on this feeling and notice that as long as you do, the eyes will stay closed. You can't open them. They are stuck together.
– Strange feeling, isn't it!

Comments: Looking upwards makes it more difficult to open the eyes as long as this position is kept. The only way to keep it for a longer time is to relax the eye muscles. Then the eyeballs will turn upwards automatically and stay there, which means hypnosis. Verbal suggestions should be given primarily in order to promote relaxation and good feelings. If a test or challenge of the patient's response is performed make it in a way that minimizes the risc for evoking resistance. The operator should appeal to willingness for cooperation and compliance. It is important to inspire the subject to keep to the suggested idea long enough to be realized. Then it is time to let the subject discover what has happened.

The question "Strange feeling, isn't it!"should be pronounced as if it is an indisputable fact that something strange has happened. A positive answer is expected, hence the exclamation mark. Do not activate critical thinking, i.e. conscious analysis and reality testing.

Finger-, hand- and arm levitation
Imagine that this finger (stroke) feels lighter so that it lifts spontaneously a couple of inches. **As soon as you have a clear mental image of this you will sense how light the finger feels.** (Already here the finger may lift) If nothing has happened continue: *A little jerk in the finger may be the first sign of change. Then an upward movement of the finger, feeling lighter. Sometimes another finger may lift but then it is difficult to know*

*which one. **It does not matter, but I would like you to be aware of any movement. -Now the index finger moved** (only if a movement has been observed).

Finger signals are very useful in dentistry. Suggestions may be like the following: **When you feel relaxed and ready for treatment you may let this finger rise (stroke). It will rise some inches automatically as a sign to me that you feel calm, relaxed and ready to let me start while you stay relaxed. You mustn't do anything. The finger will rise automatically, but not until you feel prepared to let me start the treatment that I have described and that you want. When the finger is up it means that you feel calm enough and that you want to give a signal to me to go ahead, but if you later want me to stop just lower the finger. You will have full control.** At the slightest sign of movement, comment and encourage further movement upwards.

If nothing happens within a minute continue: **To save time I will put your finger in a position where I want it. Your task will be to put it down it anything disturbs you. Is that okey? -Mm.** When you lift the finger it usually will stay up as an effect of catalepsy. You must be very cautious whatever you do, and at the same time give praise for every progress.
If the finger lowers stop immediately and don't continue until it is back again. Patients will often get used to the treatment, paired with relaxation, encouragement and praise. If you show patience and trust in your method the relaxation will deepen after a while and the treatment can be performed in an easy way.

Levitation may in many cases be a strong experience. Still stronger is maybe the experience of an arm levitation. In a dental chair it can be suitable as a continuation of glove analgesia if an extra deep trance is needed.

Glove analgesia
When potentially painful work is to be performed it may be a good strat-

egy, especially with new patients, to let them experience a suggested glove analgesia, followed by arm levitation and transmission of the analgesia from hand to cheek. The hand should be in contact with the cheek until the transmission is complete and the cheek feels numb. The fact that pain can be influenced and numbness can be achieved by psychological means sometimes needs to be demonstrated to sceptical patients. After a short induction of hypnosis you may continue like this:

When I tap on the back of your hand, it's like dead matter, wood or plaster. The skin may remind you of a thick leader glove and the hand of a foreign object, not connected to your body. As you relax more and more you can imagine that the hand is disconnected from your brain and that it feels numb. When you have noticed the change, let a finger rise as a signal to me, that I may make a test for numbness by pinching the skin. Is that okay? -Mm. When the finger has lifted: *The harder i pinch the more you relax. You are so comfortable that nothing will bother you. Maybe your finger will rise even more as you enjoy the relaxation?*
Pinch the skin while observing the subject's face. *The harder I pinch the more you relax.*

Handclasp test
Prepare the subject by telling that it is good to concentrate before relaxing and that you want to use handclasp to maximize concentration. (Show how you clasp your hands). Although this is like prayers do, now it has nothing with religion to do.

Please interlock your fingers and fold your hands like this (show). Press out as much air as possible until the hands feel like a solid unit. The borders between the hands are loosening and they are like a unit made of wood or plaster, carved or cast in one piece. It's a unit, one single piece to focus on. Enjoy the feeling of the hands becoming united, to an inseparable block. Let the fingertips press inwards and the hands will be so firmly bonded that they won't open until I say so. Now, your hands form a block. They are firmly united and it's a good feeling. They can't be separated, sticking together as they are. A good feeling of being focused.

After a positive test suggestions are given that they return to normal and feel like two hands. At the same time it is a good moment to suggest a deepening of relaxation.

Variation of the handclasp test
Fold your hands like this and stretch your index fingers so that they are pointing straight upwards and become parallel . (Show). *Look between the fingertips and feel the magnetic force pulling them together when I put my finger in the gap. Just before they meet, your eyes will feel tired and when the fingers touch each other, your eyes will close and arms relax. Very near now! Now ! Eyes closing and arms relaxing* (Grab the hands, separate them and help them down to the armchair or lap). *Arms feel heavy and eyes are comfortably closed.*

Amnesia test
Like everything else that has to do with suggestion, amnesia (inability to remember) is the result of influence from expectations and feelings. In the old days it was believed that everybody who had been in deep trance would have amnesia afterwards. Of course the operator's expectation of this was perceived by the subject and it could work as an indirect suggestion. Today it is well known that much of what earlier was characterizing the trance states was an effect of expectation. The tendency to forget certain things, i.e an appointment with the dentist is a common day problem. According to Freud it has the function to keep the awareness free from disturbing material.

If so, forgetting a dental appointment would sometimes depend on amnesia in patients with dental fear. Among these, the most prone to amnesia are the deep trance subjects. It is wise to give them suggestions to make arrangements in order to remember appointments, because it is a fact that they need help and that blaming them for forgetting will seldom help. You could also make use of their ability for amnesia by suggesting that they will only remember the positive aspects of the dental treatment. A good way of doing this is to compare with how common it is to forget things that you don't want to think about like illnesses, pain and traumatic experiences. After that give a description of what worked out well in the actual session, praise the patient and suggest positive thoughts and feelings about the next appointment.

You may then suggest that the memory of one particular experience that you know was positive will remain after the session and that everything else will fade away. In order to provoke and test amnesia the following suggestions would be used: *"When you have opened your eyes you will remember just one interesting experience. Everything else slides away from the consciousness and it will feel unimportant at the moment"*.

Suggestions of amnesia can only be expected to work if the hypnosis is fairly deep. The same applies to posthypnotic suggestions, made to the subject while in a hypnotic trance, to be acted on after emerging from trance. It is considered that a subject reacting on a post-hypnotic suggestion enters a trance, an ASC with dissociation, while performing the suggested act. Even if the suggested action is strange, like turning paintings on a wall upside down there will be complete amnesia for the moment when the suggestion was accepted. On the question why the act is made the answer will indicate this and it will be obvious that it is a rationalisation, an attempt to give an explanation, based on logic.

Hallucinations
In deep hypnosis the eyes can be open and suggested hallucinations can be experienced.
A visual imagination can become so vivid that it seems to be real. As an imagined flower is used as a focusing point in the standard induction, it could also be used as a test of the ability to hallucinate. Tell the subject to

71

stay comfortably relaxed and then add: *While the rest of your body stays relaxed, your eyes will open automatically when you are prepared to see your favorite flower in my hand. I am holding it in front of you. Tell me, what colour is it? If you want to sense how it feels to touch, just try it!* It must be added that this test has no place in the ordinary clinical work and should only be used with informed consent.

Auditory hallucinations of music can be associated with ideomotor activity by letting a finger move in line with the rhythm. As long as the finger of a dental patient moves you can assume that nothing is annoying. Auditory hallucination of music has the advantage of being attuned to what the patient likes to hear. Once I offered my patients to listen to an audiotape with popular music and told them that the idea was to replace chemical anesthesia with audio anesthesia. In case of need for more anaesthesia the patients were instructed to activate a noise sound. Earphones were put on and the music was started.

Three observations astonished me, after having treated a whole class of teenagers, using audio analgesia. Almost everybody refrained from chemical anesthesia. Nobody ever activated the noise sound. Most interesting of all was when I had once forgotten to start the music after having given instructions and put the earphones in place. Not until I was almost ready with the drilling and excavation of deep caries, I found that I had forgotten to start the audiotape. Influenced by my knowledge of the power of suggestion I supposed that the patient had heard music, although I hadn't started the tape. -How did it work, I asked the boy. -Fine, he said. I realized that he had been in trance and asked:"How was the music? – Good. – Did you feel any pain? -No! -Now there will be a little more drilling. I will offer you another kind of music. This time I started the audiotape. Everything went well and afterwards I asked: "Which music was the best?" -The first one he answered without hesitation.

Another strange thing happened when I was assisting a dental surgeon who had offered nitrous-oxide to an anxious patient. I pretended to give gas and gave relaxation suggestion which worked very well. The treatment was performed without any problems. What astonished me was that afterwards when I told the patient that he had in fact got no nitrous-oxide because he managed so well without the gas he expressed some disappointment. What can be learned from this is that you should always get an informed consent before using hypnosis or a planned placebo treatment. Nobody wants to be fooled.

The olfactory nerve leads smell signals from the nose to the olfactory bulb, close to the primitive parts of the brain that have to do with emotions. In the bulb they are processed and then will pass information about the smell to other areas closely connected to it, the so called limbic system. Aromas can trigger feelings and memories, stored deeply in the unconscious mind. If the flower, mentioned above happens to have some smell and you make a subject sense it this may deepen the trance considerably due to the associations and the regression that may take place. Deepening can also be attained by asking the subject to engage the tactile sense by asking how it feels to touch the flower..

The taste will be strongly activated in most persons if they are asked to imagine a sour lemon, cut into halves with dripping sour juice. If asked to imagine tasting the juice by licking the lemon this will probably cause salivation. Taste experiences are closely related to aromas and can, like other suggestions focus the attention which leads to a deeper trance. In dentistry many materials taste and smell. In some patients they have been connected with unease through conditioning. This indicates that the senses of taste and smell should be engaged in the hypnotic treatment.

In deep trance it is possible to suggest erasure of certain perceptions from the environment. The phenomena is called negative hallucination. Taste and smell sensations can be blocked and in dentistry or surgery it is obvious that suggested ansthesia is a favorable negative hallucination in cases where it works. The problem is that it is not as predictable as the effect of general anesthesia and therefore it is not much used.

Suggestion is a strange factor that guides people's behaviours more than logic and more than most people realize. It is a totally unconscious influence. The aim of conscious suggesting is to release reflexes and behaviours, that are not consciously controlled. In animals you can often see a primitive mass reaction, where one and the same behaviour is triggered by a signal. The response may be a fear reaction, but it may also be a well established pattern of reflexive imitation.

In humans similar primitive reflexive reactions exist, disconnected from logic and reason. They are direct, spontaneous, well established and may be the result of suggestion. Examples of mass-suggestion can be found in football arenas and pop concerts. Very distasteful exemples from other areas are lynching and mobbing. Some common idea among persons with similar mental maps has stirred up emotions of hate, rage or fear. These are spread by imitation and the feelings become stronger, which calls for action. As soon as somebody or something is found or invented as a goal for action, the risk for impulsive unpremeditated and violent action is high. Critical thinking is bypassed.

How focus on an idea can trigger a response has been studied by the Frenchman Emile Coué. He meant that self- suggestion was a good way of influencing oneself in order to reach the own positive goals. In the 1920ies he became famous all over the world for his ideas. His book *Self Mastery through Conscious Autosuggestion* gives examples of how the most varying afflictions and problems were cured with suggestion. The text can be found on the internet. Coué emphasized that all suggestions utmost are self suggestions. His theories are well formulated in the book *Suggestion and Autosuggestion* by Charles Baudoin, 1923. The language is a little old fashioned and small changes have been made in the next chapter of this book.

13. Coué's laws of suggestion. Ideomotor and ideosensory effect

1. The Law of Concentrated Attention
If spontaneous attention is concentrated on an idea, this tends to become realized.

2. The Law of Auxiliary Emotion, also called the *Law of dominant effect*
When a suggestion is supported by emotion it will become stronger than every other suggestion, given at the same moment.

3. The Law of Reversed Effort
If conscious will is in conflict with phantasy, the phantasy will win.

4. The Law of Subconscious Teleology
When the goal has been traced out the unconscious will find out how to reach it.
"When the end has been suggested the subconscious finds means for its realisation." (Baudouin, 1920: 117).

Comments on law nr 1. *The Law of Concentrated Attention:*
If spontaneous attention is concentrated on an idea, this tends to become realized.
Ideas upon which attention becomes focused become correspondingly magnified in their effect. Spontaneous autosuggestions may capture the

attention automatically. Conscious autosuggestions must be repeated with mental focus, and with certainty and faith in them. This obviously resembles Braid's definition of hypnotism as focused attention upon a dominant idea ("monoideism").

An idea involving some change or action may catch attention and be realized immediately, which is an effect of spontaneous autosuggestion. Conscious autosuggestions as well as hetero suggestions must be in focus long enough to be accepted as a goal. The time factor is important. The suggestion must be in focus and is usually repeated. The change or goal should be clearly imagined. This can be demonstrated with the suggestibility tests. All of these build primarily on law #1.

The word spontaneous implies involvement of emotion. Another crucial factor is of course the restriction of disturbing stimuli. This applies both to outer and inner stimuli. To the latter belongs activity in the brain cortex, i.e. logical or critical thinking and worrying. According to Coué a suggested idea triggers unconscious work and after a certain time the idea becomes realized. The "work" can be regarded as associations to images that help to make the primary image more distinct and that also arouse emotions. The emotions help to keep the target image in fokus until it becomes accepted.

A simple test of suggestibility doesn't seem to be able to evoke much emotion. The question is how to make it interesting enough to keep a suggested idea in focus? In heterosuggestion the answer may be found in the fact that the will to cooperate with, and to please a person, who has been accepted as a leader is known to be a strong motivational factor, as it generates a need to comply.

When a suggestion is presented, it is intended to result in an image of what could be expected to happen. In order to make the image clear the suggestion is repeated several times letting no other ideas intrude the mental scene. The attention should be continuously lingering on the suggested idea. The only guarantee for this is that energy is available, which in this context means emotion. Coué emphasized that it takes time for suggestions to gain strength, i.e. to become loaded with energy or become accepted as Coué used to say. A comparison with the psychological term motivation is near at hand. Coué meant that a suggestion that is accepted will seek to become realized. Thus it has become a psychological drive, a motive.

In self- suggestion it may be a problem to keep focus on a consciously selected suggestion, as spontaneity may be lacking. There is a risk that unwanted ideas and imaginations may pop up. Inspiration in all forms to use self suggestion can be helpful and putting oneself into a comfortable, relaxed hypnotic state makes it easier to link a good, calm feeling to the self suggestion, that should be repeated several times in order to prevent other idéas from coming up.

Important mechanisms are ideomotor and ideosensoric effect. The ideomotor effect means that muscles become involuntarily activated by imaginations involving muscular activity. The activity may be regarded as unconsciously triggered reflexes as a response to lively cognitions. The whole body posture can be influenced. Our body language often reflects our innermost thoughts and feelings. That is an effect of ideomotor activity. A typical example is that when you listen to somebody telling opinions that you completely agree with you may nod your head more or less unconsciously. In roleplaying focus is on inner pictures and the actor makes use of ideomotor and ideosensory effect.

It is important for people working with clinical hypnosis to observe ideomotor activity, since it gives a clue to the degree of suggestibility as well as to the subject's involvement in imaginations. Finger signals are very useful for communicating with a person in hypnosis without disturbing the trance. If a patient is given the suggestion that a finger will come up as a sign that he feels ready for the treatment you can rely on the answer.

Either the finger will lift and then it is appropriate to start the treatment, or nothing happens with the finger. In that case you have the possibility to find out what obstacles there are and how to eliminate them.

After the suggestion that a finger will move upwards, an image of this is formed in the brain. This image is processed after associations, that may be either spontaneous or triggered by new suggestions, and then it may be accepted. If the patient feels ready it will, in an unconscious way, activate muscles that make the finger move upwards. The finger will move without conscious, volitional influence. The movement can be stopped, but if motivation for taking own initiatives is lacking, which usually is the case, the finger will continue upwards. Many patients have reported a feeling of being influenced by an almost magical force, that they didn,t steer consciously or influence in any way. They may think that it is fantastic.

Ideomotor activity is not regulated by the autonomic nerve system but by the peripheral nerve system, in the same way as behaviours that we have learned to perform without thinking. Examples of such are walking, breaking a car or a bicycle or playing an instrument or writing, when it has been automated after a lot of training.

If you imagine that you bite in a sour lemon it may cause saliva production, an ideosensoric response in taste buds and salivary glands. To suggest analgesia, it may be sufficient to remind of the sensation when some part of the body has become anesthetized. If that experience is lacking most people have experienced that an arm or leg has become numb due to sustained pressure on a nerve. By focusing on the memory of the sensation this can be revoked, which is an example of ideosensoric effect.

Comments on law #2
Law of dominant effect. When a suggestion is supported by an emotion, it will become stronger than every other suggestion, given at the same moment.

When, for one reason or another, an idea is enveloped in a powerful emotion, there is more likelihood that this idea will be suggestively realised." (Baudouin, 1920: 114). The auxiliary role of emotion in capturing attention and transforming an idea into bodily action is a key feature of spontaneous negative autosuggestion. Negative ideas stick in our minds because of the powerful emotions attached to them, especially the emotion of fear.

Baudouin stresses that this gives spontaneous autosuggestion a kind of initial advantage, as many people implicitly recognise, because our deliberate attempts at conscious autosuggestion are unlikely to be accompanied by such strong and sincere emotion.

Emotions play an important role when it comes how to catch, guide and focus attention. It may be caught by suggestions that are suited to the patient's actual needs. In clinical settings the patient is often worried and insecure. Calming, reassuring and relaxing suggestions will be supported by the patient's current needs. Therefore a change of the emotional environment can shift from anxiety to great calmness almost instantly.

One emotion has in this case inhibited another emotion of the opposite quality. When a shift from anxiety to calmness has occurred the new emotion will be quite stable, but to maintain it, calming suggestions may have to be repeated. The desire to follow instructions and to cooperate is heightened in hetero hypnosis. This is perhaps the strongest emotional factor that give support to the operators suggestions. Emotional responses can be conditioned so that as soon the operator lays his/her arm on the patients shoulder this triggers a calm feeling.

The inclination to suit an operator and the willingness to cooperate and to focus on what is suggested characterizes hetero hypnosis. Wolpe launched the theory of reciprok inhibition, meaning the same as Coué's law #2, namely that an idea that spontaneous attention is focusing on, pushes away every other idea. In the meantime it becomes loaded with emotional energy. It becomes paired with a positive feeling until it becomes an accepted suggestion. That means that a person enjoying relaxation and calmness cannot experience unease or <u>suffer</u> from pain at the same time. An example of how impossible it is to focus attention on more than one thing at a time is demonstrated by so-called mentalists who, by using distraction, can pick peoples belongings from their pockets without them noticing it.

Wolpe's theory that the pairing of an anxiety provoking stimulus with calming stimuli will weaken the association between the original stimulus and anxiety indicates that there is an antagonistic effect between the emotions. He called it reciprocal inhibition. Coué means that calming suggestions not only weaken anxiety, they abolish it when they become linked with an idea of comfort and ease and that nothing bothers as an accepted suggestion.

In advertising it is common to try to present a product together with something that is known to arouse positive feelings. Cars have been presented with young, good looking, happy and sexy people. Cigarettes are smoked in beautiful, fresh nature och and certain drinks are shown by young, good looking, smiling people, having fun in a party. Sometimes even material that evokes negative emotions is used for attracting attention, a primary goal.

In the induction of hypnosis a slightly negative emotion of confusement and unsecurity can be created in the beginning by giving suggestions that are difficult to interpret. That is to create a need for certainty. If unambiguous, positive, simple and distinct suggestions follow their probability of being accepted has been enhanced. The majority of dental patients already feel a certain stress which makes them susceptible to calming suggestions.

Giving suggestions means evoking idéas and imaginations, hoping that they will be accepted as goals. As mentioned before, the idéas need emotional support. The fact that humans are social creatures, striving for good relationships means that this is an important factor in many situations. A positive relation between the hypnotist and the subject will facilitate the acceptance of suggestions.

In fact, if the relation is good and the atmosphere is favorable a doctor, dentist or hygienist aiming at provoking relaxation and analgesia in a patient doesn't need to do much to reach this goal. Just suggesting that it may be more comfortable having the eyes closed, and feel free to think about a pleasant memory will often be enough. If the patient follows the suggestion it is important not to disturb the inner experience by talking of other things.

Comments on law #3.
The Law of Reversed Effort.
Internal conflict occurs between the will and imagination, but the imagination is always stronger.

The law of reversed effort raises a second obstacle to the use of auto suggestion because the more we try to consciously struggle with a dominant idea the more powerful its effects become. "When an idea imposes itself on the mind to such an extent as to give rise to a suggestion, all the conscious efforts which the subject makes in order to counteract this suggestion are not merely without the desired effect, but they actually run counter to the subject's conscious wishes and tend to intensify the suggestion." (Baudouin, 1920: 116). He elaborates this by describing the law of reversed effect as exemplified by the self-antagonistic attitude of mind that says, "I would like to... but I *cannot*." This notion might be seen as similar to the modern technique of "reverse psychology", a persuasion technique which aims, paradoxically, to persuade someone to accept an idea by suggesting the opposite to it.

When somebody wants to achieve something, but has got an unfavourable imagination of possible failure this imagination is stronger than the will.

It is striking to see when a person, sceptical to hypnosis, easily goes into trance after it has be demonstrated that other forces than willpower, i.e. ideomotor effect or catalepsy are stronger than the outspoken scepticism. Many times, especially in persons with addiction, it is obvious that their promise to stop the misuse is not reliable if supported only by willpower. What a person claims to be willing to do weighs lightly against the emotional forces and tempting images that determines what actually is done.

Other idéas and imaginations, in conflict with the wanted ones, may catch attention and get a suggestive influence. An example of this is when the will to fall asleep is counteracted by the fear of not being able to sleep. The latter thought is so frightening that it becomes stronger than any other suggestion. Effort to sleep just makes the problem worse. The dominating suggestion is: "You can't sleep!" The more you try the more impossible it becomes. This is an example of the law of the reversed effort.

Coué's own recipe of how to avoid using effort of will in auto suggestion was to repeat a favorable suggestion twenty times without thinking or straining oneself. He also found that after using specific suggestions it was good to end up with more general ones. A famous example of this is the self suggestion: " Day by day in every way I' m getting better and better.

When giving suggestions to a client it is good to choose a theme and then start with generally held suggestions encourage clear and detailed imagination. According to Coué, suggestions should be like painting descriptions, in order to promote a vivid imagination. It is wise to be aware of the fact that you never know exactly what subjects imagine. By asking questions about details you can stimulate them to make their own images more vivid with engagement of as many senses as possible.

An effective method of influencing is to use metaphors. For example the feeling of heaviness in the legs can be boosted by giving a painting description of a pair of tree trunks lying heavily and immobile on a river bank, after an overflow. They weigh tons after a long time in the water and now they are stuck in the ground, and seem impossible to move . They must be very heavy indeed.

The word fantasy means the capability to produce pictures, imaginations, memories on the inner scene together with the associated feelings. In the ordinary waking state these pictures are sketchy and not rich of details. That is not necessary if they are used just for the purpose of orientation in the environment. When it comes to an ASC, focus is much more on details with all the five senses involved. Attention then becomes more focused, evokes more feeling and therefore tends to stay where it is.

Imagination is one of the most important factors of hypnosis. It may give rise either to a spontaneous suggestion, formed without reality testing or, if it is a consciously planned suggestion it may be used to influence and motivate for a desired change. Focusing on a specific image and letting no other images intrude consciousness reminds of James Braid's term monoideism. The image should be rich of details and the attention on it should be free from effort. Repetition and passivity are important factors.

Comments on law #4.
The Law of Subconscious Teleology (Efficiency in achieving goal)
When a goal has been accepted the unconscious will find the means to reach it.

"When the end has been suggested the subconscious finds means for its realisation." (Baudouin, 1920: 117). Autosuggestion therefore focuses upon the goal and allows the mind to spontaneously find its own means to achieve that goal. It is true that this attitude seems conducive to auto suggestion, though it should be qualified by adding that in terms of complex or long-term goals it is usually advisable to break them down into steps and stages because the mind sometimes has a limited ability to work out solutions spontaneously.

In dentistry and medical practice the primary goal is to make the patient relax and therefore a suggestion to see him/herself completely calm and relaxed in the dental chair could be helpful, if given at the right time. Believe in the patient's capability to be influenced by suggestion! Today there is unfortunately an overconfidence in medicine and a lack of knowledge of the power of suggestion in the medical field. Calming suggestions and the use of well suited and repeated goal pictures to a patient in a state of pleasant relaxation may deepen trance and sometimes give a long lasting, relaxing and calming effect.

An operator using hypnosis must be able to assess suggestibility and, if it is high enough, to believe in the power of suggestion. If having an own phobia of pain it will be difficult to convey, in a convincing manner, the idéa that pain can be abolished threw mental mechanisms or that it could be totally disregarded when one is relaxed and knows that pain signals are quite unimportant, as they have no message. It happens that dental patient think that pain should be reported. For them it may be relaxing to hear that they don't have to register pain and that it is better itf they focus on some pleasant imagination or memory.

The goal picture shows the end result of a suggestion, before it has become realized. To see and experience other people, that are deeply hypnotized, may facilitate the creation of a goal picture. For some people group hypnosis works especially well. If a subject has been hypnotized earlier or has witnessed hypnosis he/she has an imagination or expectation of what is going to happen. If sleep is expected the hypnotic behaviour will maybe be like that of sleeping and then there may be an expectation of a wakening procedure.

When making a suggestibility test you can chose to describe what will happen or you can suggest the goal as if it is already a fact. If you do so, you should have some indication of that it may be true. Then it may be worded like this: *" Your arm is heavy and immobile. It is like united with the armchair and it weighs a lot. It's heavy and immobile. Can't be lifted. Weighing too much to move. It is linked with the armchair, completely stuck there."* If the operator fears to lose his/her face the risk could be reduced by giving a painting description of what possibly may be felt. Exemple:*" Your arm is lying on the armchair and feels heavier and heavier, the more it becomes relaxed. You could imagine that it is heavy as lead, weighing tons. Maybee you feel that it is extremely heavy, connected with the armchair like glued to it and pressing down on it ?"*

Coué proceeded methodically when he taught self suggestion. He worked with the sway test. Subjects were trained to be passive and he let them discover how the balance was influenced by their own imaginations. He let them pronounce self suggestions of falling forwards or backwards and then gave them the hand clasp test. (Chapter 12)

The Method of Conscious Autosuggestion

Text from Charles, Baudouin's book Suggestion och Autosuggestion 1924
Therefore every time that you have a pain, physical or otherwise, you will go quietly to your room (it is better if you can do this, but you can do it also in the middle of the road if necessary), but if you go to your room, sit down and shut your eyes, pass your hand lightly across your forehead if it is mental distress, or upon the part that hurts if it is a pain in any part of the body, and repeat the words: It is going, it is going, etc. Very rapidly, even at the risk of gabbling, it is of no importance. The essential idea is to say: it is going, it is going, so quickly, that it is impossible for a thought of contrary nature to force itself between the words.

Nice relaxation (brings) calm sleep. Repeat 50-100 times!

14. Preparing for hypnosis. Induction principles

You should make the patient believe in you and create a positive expectation of your professional skills. Your prestige as an expert in the field you are working in, together with a positive emotional clima will create a so-called yes set. This is the basis for rapport, which means a state that occurs when two people feel that they are truly able to connect with and communicate with one another. It is usually based on shared values and a common interest. This feeling can be promoted through mutual attention, positivity and ongoing eye contact, matching breathing rhythms and mirroring body postures.

Intrinsic motivation refers to behaviours that are driven by internal rewards. When you notice that your own values are the same as the patient's, show this and when they differ do nothing at all. Inner motivation is often rooted in early life experiences that lead to life rules and so called schemas. These are examples of the inner mapping and they influence how information is interpreted and make memories change over time. Intrinsic motivation may create resistance against hypnosis. In that case take it away by defining your method as nothing but relaxation.

The operators conduct should be kind, confident, empathetic, reassuring and clarifying. Before the first induction of hypnosis the value of relaxation (hypnosis) should be explained and the patient should be asked for the permission to let the operator give a short instruction. This should be made professionally, without hesitation. For beginners it is recommended to use a standard induction that has been well trained. Don't use the word hypnosis initially because it may raise false expectations. It is better to talk about the ability to relax during treatment. Be calm and objective and use a normal pitch of voice. It is important that the patient is positive to the idea of using a few minutes for relaxation training.

Make this short, simple and natural. An induction should be tailored to the clinical situation and be free from mysticism and dominance. Some patients will go in a spontaneous trance if you merely ask them to shut their eyes and relax. That applies especially those who have been hypnotized before. Hypnosis in dentistry can be seen as a state of deep relaxation, combined with the tendency and willingness to cooperate which is typical when the rapport is good. If you want to exercise to make inductions with a friend or relative you can't count on the prestige factor. You may talk about a relaxation exercise and an occasion to learn something useful.

The ability to relax can, to a certain degree be trained, but it also depends on the inborn quality of suggestibility. Not everybody is capable of going into a deep state of relaxation and to remain there. Luckily enough this is not always necessary. If there is no deep relaxation the important thing is to avoid working on a tense patient. The training should aim at teaching passivity and to avoid tensing any muscles. Calming mental imaginations may be easier to concentrate on than physical relaxation.

A focusing point, often offered at the beginning of an induction is the tension in some part of the body. The idea is that it is easier to focus on something that is already there than on something that you want to suggest (relaxation). The muscle will get tired and then suggestions of relaxation will be easily accepted. If the tension is also manifested in some disturbing mental activity, an attempt to stop this should be made by stimulating a passive attitude. The desired mental activity could be compared with an image of a breathless surface of a lake when it is windstill at dawn and everything is calm.

 In the ordinary everyday waking state of consciousness, the brain cortex is active. Judgements and decisions are made, logic reasoning is going on and different alternatives of behaviour are evaluated by means of reality testing. Ideas lacking of support from obvious facts will in most cases be sorted out before they influence the behaviour. A conscious choice of behaviour is made. In the hypnotic state the major part of the brain cortex is at rest and logic, analytical reasoning is put on the back burner.

The first step of a hypnosis induction is usually to ask the subject to focus on something special. The outgoing attention is thereby restricted and monotony may be used to exhaust it and give room for inner experiences. Spontaneous attention may be attracted by some body sensation, (local awareness) or by an image popping up on the mental scene after some suggestions. The mentioning of what could be expected i.g. a flower, a well known face, an animal, a natural scenery or a hobby activity increases the chances that some image will become realized.

Instead of using monotony, the spontaneous attention may be caught from the very beginning. That is the most effective way of narrowing the field of attention. Conscious muscular and mental activities are blocked and replaced by the experience of unconsciously guided bodily sensations, or mental imagery. These will be the only sensations available, except for the operators voice. Involuntary reflexes like breathing, pulse, blinking and cataleptic immobility, which are normally unconscious, will easily come into awareness and so will certain images.

Comments should be made on visible signs of relaxation like eye closure, disappearance of wrinkles in the face, tilting of the head to the side, the feet resting in parallel on the heels, moving the forefeet outwards. Every reflex is worth paying attention to and if it is a sign of increasing relaxation, positive comments should be given. Ideomotor and ideo sensory sensations are focusing points that should be utilized, because these phenomena often make a deep impression and deepen hypnosis.

A classical induction of hypnosis, according to Braid, is initiated by having the subject look steadily at a shiny object. The blink reflex is commented and suggestions about increasing heaviness of the eyelids are repeated, together with the suggestion that as soon as they have closed the subject will go into a hypnotic sleep. Even if such an induction may be effective it is not suited for a dental clinic. Patients will be more motivated to cooperate if they are offered control of what is happening. Only a few of them expect to sleep why it is, in most cases, better to talk about a deep, nice and comfortable state of relaxation.

A person who is offered hypnosis (relaxation) for the first time could be motivated for a concentration test by being told that focusing ability is important for relaxation. In social context people often have a divided attention. In a conversation they not only listen to what is said but a great deal of their attention is focusing on reading body language in order to evaluate emotional content and trustworthiness. The same process takes place when a concentration task is given. The subjects concentration is usually only supported by willpower and the attention will split automatically.

For the purpose of hypnosis, the emotionally guided attention is the interesting part and the willpowered focus should be weakened and passified during induction. Characteristic for hypnosis is the tendency to linger on every single experience. The reason is that it is an emotional state with calm and stable feelings.

Suggestions to focus on interesting details, without making any effort, will readily be followed. Passivity combined with presence in the present like in mindfulness could be suggested. What usually happens is that focus spontaneously tend to linger on some physical sensation, usually a feeling of heaviness and warmth in the limbs. When that has happened praise should be given for the obvious focusing skills.

Although a primarily call for effort to concentrate is made, it is communicated on another, emotional level that it is better, more comfortable and more efficient just to experience with an open mind what is going on. To avoid making efforts attention is directed to spontaneous reflexes in the form of immobility, heaviness, relaxation, calm feelings and slow breathing.

15. Three simple inductions suitable for practicing with subject sitting in a comfortable dental chair

A. **This induction builds on the tests of arm catalepsy, arm lowering and arm heaviness. (Page 65) If you are not working with dentistry just omit the last part.**

Wording and description
Most people have a tendency to tense up, so if it is okay with you I would like to show you how you can relax quickly and easily. May I? – Mm. Okey! Please follow my instructions: Take a deep breath! Breathe in soundly and at the same time <u>rise the subjects hand</u> a little bit up from the armchair or lap. *Hold it, hold it and notice the tension in your chest and arm.* When the uplifted hand is cataleptic let go of it. Continue: *Exhale and relax the <u>rest</u> of your body. Imagine that your hand is resting on a floating, magic pillow. It begins to sink and shrink and your hand, resting heavily on it goes down and you get more and more relaxed all over at the same time. You won't be totally relaxed until the pillow has collapsed and your hand has reaches the armchair. Deeper and deeper relaxed as the hand sinks down.* Give time enough to let the arm sink at its own pace. When it reaches the armchair or lap: *The arm is heavy as lead* (stroke from shoulder to hand) Lift it after a little while and drop it. Give praise if it falls passively. You could stimulate the phantasy by comparing with a wet dish rag. Continue: *Now take a deep breath and feel the relaxation going like a wave threw your whole body when you*

exhale. Now instruct the patient to focus on the arm heaviness. **While you feel the heaviness in your arm I will help you to open your mouth and put it in comfortable position.** Lower the chin and ask the patient to open even more. *Perfect! Mouth wide open without effort! Feel how comfortable – it is in perfect balance..*

B. Wick's induction with subject sitting in upright position on an ordinary chair.
Let me show you how quickly and easily you can relax? May I? – OK

Instruction to the subject	Behaviour of the operator and further suggestions
Take a deep breath and hold it!	Breathe in soundly and raise the subject's arm straight up.
Hold it !, hold it !, hold it !	Release the arm gently so that it remains in that position.
Exhale and let the <u>rest</u> of your body relax	Andas ut hörbart
Now the arm will start to relax	Deep relaxation won't come until the arm has come all the way down.
The arm will begin to sink down	Give praise as soon as it starts to sink.
It feels heavier and heavier	I will help it to find a comfortable position on your lap
Wants to rest comfortably.	Place the arm comfortably and stroke from the shoulder to the hand.
Heavy and slack	Stroke.
The arm is heavy! Breathe calmly and enjoy!	Attune your own breathing

C. Relaxation induction

If you want to initiate relaxation in a very natural way you can seek the patient's permission to use some minutes for relaxation training. Start with suggesting that the eyes should be closed. Then continue: With the eyes closed you may notice some tensions in the body. Focus on them and notice how they change and especially how it feels when they relax. Listen to my voice and I will help you to relax.

Breathe in deeply, hold it. Think of the tensions and feel how you relax when you exhale. Now! Let go and relax! Take a new deep breath! Hold it! Exhale and relax. Breathe in! (pause) *Breathe out! Now, allow the breathing to find its own rhythm. Meanwhile, your face is relaxing. The eyelids are comfortably closed. Just let all the tiny muscles around them relax completely. The eyeballs will automatically turn upwards when all the muscles around them relax. The eyelids feel tightly and firmly closed and they continue to relax until they feel like they won't open. The muscles around them are completely relaxed and, at the moment, out of function. You can try to open the eyes but the eyelids will feel like glued and won't open. That is a good sign that you are doing well. Cheeks and lips are at rest and feels heavy. The tongue is relaxed. Neck muscles get limp and loose. The belly and the back relax. Every breath brings more relaxation and belly breathing is slow and relaxing. The legs become heavy as a pair of timber trunks. You breathe in and out. In and out. In and out.* (attune to subject's breathing) *The breathing goes on automatically. Nothing must be done, just enjoy relaxing. When I lift your arm you can imagine that it feels like a wet, sloppy dish rag that falls down passively when i drop it. Very relaxed. Just continue to enjoy the relaxation, the calmness and the heaviness of your arm.*

16. Norrsell's standard induction (https://youtu.be/OvYeNbW-B6I)

The following induction of hypnosis is well suited to general dental and medical praxis. Begin with telling the patient why you want to show how to relax. You may have noticed tension in the hands or in the face, where perspiring is also a sign of tension. Scared, watchful eyes or other body language may indicate anxiety and tension. Patients also may tell the operator that they feel scared. All these signs are indications for relaxation.

Some patient see a proposal of relaxation as something that may prolong the unpleasant situation. Then you should inform them that you just need a couple av minutes to induce relaxation and that then you will start immediately to get things done. Tell that it will be a relaxing experience because you will do everything you can to make it so. It is important to get the patient's permission before you start.

- *To relax you must be able to concentrate. Can you imagine a flower? It will be easier if you shut the eyes. Have you chosen flower? – Mm!*

- *Think about what characteristics you see, what feeling it arouses, if you like it and if it is enjoying life? How are the surroundings? Meanwhile I'll put your arm in an upright position.* Lift and put the elbow on the armchair with the lower arm in an upright position. Now use non-verbal suggestions to convey the idea that it should remain in its position. <u>Release</u> as soon as possible, and if it moves put it back firmly until it stays and becomes cataleptic. That is the goal. Therefore it is important that you d<u>on't hold on to the am too long.</u>

- *Notice this!* Tap the wrist a few times to test for catalepsy. Comment your observations in a positive way. For example: *The arm has found a balance,* or *-returns back every time I dislocate it by tapping on it,* or *– is rigid. You notice that, don't you?* Say this in a firm tone, indicating that you expect a positive answer. Only tell the truth about the degree of catalepsy or, if there is no catalepsy, just comment on that as if it is a progress that he arm already has begun to relax.

- *In a moment I will put it down on the armchair and it will become heavy and relaxed.* Wait at least ten seconds. It is very important to give time for the suggestion to be fully accepted. When the arm has been laid down, stroke it from the shoulder to the hand and say: *Heavy! Now allow the arm to become more and more relaxed and heavy while you can feel free to think of the flower or some memory that feels good. The arm is heavy.* Sometimes this will be enough, but often a deepening of trance is recommendable. Continue by focusing on arm heaviness and finger levitation.

When your arm feels so heavy that it is like one with the armchair, pressing down with its heaviness you may find that it is like glued or tied to the arm rest. At the same time this forefinger (stroke it) *begins to feel lighter and lighter until it raises automatically as a sign, that the arm is firmly anchored.* (Observe and comment signs of tension or movement in the finger). *I don't know how long it will take until you feel ready for treatment but the finger won't come up until the arm feels extremely heavy and relaxed.* Give further suggestions of comfort and warmth in the arm.

After a minute, if no levitation has occurred: *You may continue to relax your arm, but to save time and to know that you accept my treatment, I want this finger to be elevated as a sign that everything is OK. You may readily lower the finger if anything disturbs you and I will stop immediately. You have full control.* Lift the patient's right forefinger and ask him /her to let it stay up as a signal "go ahead" as long as nothing bothers and the arm continues to feel heavy and relaxed.

Further comments on the standard induktion
New beginners may want to read the suggestions, but it is far better to suggest without reading. You should be aware of the outlines: 1) Test of concentration, 2) characteristics of the flower, 3) arm catalepsy affirmed by patient, 4) arm heaviness. It is not necessary to use the exact wording, but it is good to ty to follow the original and to be aware of the goal of each step.

The flower is used as as a concentration test and is also a way of diverting attention, hoping that the flower will evoke associations that give positive feelings, which is usually the case. If not, you could propose something else with the patient's help. Ask for details of the image such as sounds, smells, colours and structure of materials that may be sensed? A good question is what kind of feelings the picture evokes?

While focus is still on the image a new moment is added when the arm is lifted and put in an upright position on the armchair. This makes the spontaneous go to the arm, which automatically becomes a little cataleptic when released. If it is not released it will, in many cases, start to relax and that is not intended. You want to test catalepsy and you want to know if there is a yes set in the patient. The answer to your question is crucial. If there is any hesitation in the patient it means that the critical thinking is still active and you should refrain from giving further suggestions. The best you can do is then to lay down the arm and just ask the patient to relax it. No other suggestions should be given.

Verbal comments should not be made until assessment of the grade of catalepsy and possibly some rigidity has been made by tapping on the raised lower arm. These should give a correct description of your observations. When these are reality founded and objective, one could expect a positive answer to the question, do you notice that? If a counter-question is made like: "How do you mean?" you can make the conclusion that suggestions are not effective. Just say that you want to eliminate unnecessary tensions in the arm. Put it down and give the task to keep it relaxed so that it feels comfortable. It usually works even in patients that are classified as low suggestible. But, suggestions of extreme heaviness wont work.

If the question regarding catalepsy has got an positive answer the next step should be prepared, first by describing it and then by allowing a fairly long time to pass before the arm is moved and laid on tha armchair. Take it by the wrist, lift it up, put your hand under the elbow and soften the muscles by moving the patient's hand in a circle. As soon it lies on the armchair further suggested of relaxation should be given.

Finger levitation deepens trance and at the same time it gives control. When a levitation starts it should be observed and commented directly to stimulate it. If it is only very little you could tell the patient that as you see a positive sign you would like to start a gentle treatment. "If something would be annoying just lower the finger. It will be easier for me to see the finger if it is higher up so I put it here (lift) and your only task is to lower it if you want a pause."

17. Dave Elman's induction, here adjusted to treatment of bruxism (*https://www.youtube.com/watch?v=W5rXsq3ZL9o*)

Rationale: *Independently of the cause of bruxism, it is a harmful behaviour that can be cured with hypnosis and self hypnosis. Regular relaxation exercise is helpful and I want to show you how to go into a very deep state of relaxation so that you get an idea of how it feels. Good feelings have the potential to counteract tension, stress and anxiety that use to trigger bruxism. Any questions?* Start by asking the patient to massage the cheeks and knead the jaw muscles. The eyes are open.

Enlarged and sore jaw muscles is a sign of hyperactivity. I want you to knead them until they feel limp and loose, limp and slack. Continue to massage your cheeks until they get warm and relaxed. Imagine that the jaw muscles are getting so slack that they feel elongated, comfortable and relaxed. Kneading the jaw muscles make them relax. You can make them feel warm and free from tension like long, slack ropes. There is an interspace between the upper and lower jaws. That is a sign of relaxation in the jaw muscles. Now gape like me (show) *to stretch the muscles and then relax even more. Keep a comfortable feeling of warmth in your cheeks.*

Now I want to show you how to relax your face and I begin with all the little muscles around the eyelids and let them relax to the point where they become temporarily disabled. Look at me! (Close your eyes and show *that they won't open when they are relaxed).* **As long as I focus on keeping them relaxed they won't open.**

Please shut your eyes, relax all the muscles around them until your eyelids feel tightly and firmly closed. When all the little muscles around the eyelids feel completely relaxed, they will be steadily and firmly closed, as if glued together. Comfortably and firmly closed. They are stuck. Now – test for yourself. It is impossible to open the eyes as long as you focus on the relaxation. Very well, now you can open the eyes. After this preliminary test I want to show you how to relax the whole face and body.

Take a deep breath! Let go, close the eyes and double your relaxation. (repeat a couple of times). **The eye lids are comfortably closed. They become more and more relaxed and then the relaxation spreads to the eyeballs. These will automatically roll upwards as if looking from the inside of the skull towards the top. The small tiny muscles around the eyelids are very relaxed. They are inactivated and so tightly closed that they feel like glued together and impossible to open. They are stuck.**

At the same time there is a gap between the upper and the lower jaw. If you focus entirely on both relaxation and this gap, the muscles can not be active. As long as you are totally focusing on relaxation, there is no risk that you bite together. The chin is hanging loosely.

When your face is all over relaxed, take a deep breath and relax from head to toe. (Breathe yourself in audibly, then say): **Now breathe out** (puff out audibly) **and relax. You breathe calmly in and out.** (Pacing the words in and out to the patient's breathing rate).

Your arm is so relaxed and heavy that when I lift and drop it, it falls like a wet dish rag. Each time it lands, a reflex is triggered, a wave of relaxation that goes through the entire body from top to toe.
In order to get a really deep relaxation, you also need to relax mentally.

I ask you to count the numbers loudly from 100 backwards and say: deeper relaxed after each count. The numbers tend to disappear. Let it happen! It's good that they do! You can start counting now.

- 100, deeper relaxed. ***Relax the mind!***
- 99, deeper relaxed. ***The numbers feel insignificant, fade away***
- 98, deeper relaxed. ***The thoughts are as quiet as a mirroring water surface.***
- Ninety ? (hesitates) ***Relax! Enjoy total rest of mind and body! Are the numbers gone?***
- Yes . If they are not, lift the patient's arm and suggest: ***When I drop the arm the number will disappear!***

You are now relaxed both, muscularly and mentally. Breathe in deeply and double the relaxation when you breath out. (Repeat). *Your arms are relaxed and heavy. You feel calm. Imagine looking threw a round hole in the skull. You can feel free like a bird and can fly out while the body is resting here. As in a dream, you can experience that you come to a place you associate with peace, harmony and wellbeing. You are completely free. The place you end up at may evoke feelings of recognition, joy, security, balance, or other positive feelings.*

An index finger will signal when you are there by lifting. Now your finger is becoming lighter! (As soon as there is a sign of this) *You can either see yourself as in a movie or you can feel and experience what it's like to be in place. Notice the sounds, colours and sensations and good feelings. Enjoy being in your favorite place. It makes you feel good and when the pleasant feeling is really strong your index finger raises even higher.* When it goes further up touch the cheeks and say the words: **Good feeling. *Just enjoy!***

In the future you will easily find the good feeling just by touching your cheeks and by focusing on your favorite place. We are now ready and you can feel that the positive feelings of the past become one with the present. Return to the present, orient yourself to your body and to the here and now feeling good. If you want you may stretch your arms. (Meet the eyes with a smile). Keep in mind that at this moment the suggestibility is very high. Watch your words. *You can return to the positive feeling at later times by just putting the hands on your cheeks and focus on good feelings.*

The above is just a suggestion of how to treat bruxism. In this area, much research is required. Hypnosis has been successfully used to change adverse and harmful behaviours in other areas such as thumb sucking, nail biting, stuttering, bed wetting, etc. so now it is high time to realize that it is a powerful method also in treating bruxism. Deep relaxation is beneficial but it may need to be complemented by specific measures? In the example above, initially massage of cheeks and stretching of jaw muscles was used.

Positive feelings were enhanced with the help of a memory with safe, good feelings. These we anchored to (associated with) touching the cheeks. To accomplish the above, experience is required. Below is an example of a short induction that can be used for self hypnosis. It has similarities to autogenous training.

Short induction for the treatment of bruxism with self-hypnosis.
Preparatory measures: Lie comfortably. Massage or rub your cheeks until they feel warm and comfortable. Keep this feeling and repeat the following self-suggestion ten times: *The cheeks feel warm and comfortable.* Make the mouth wide open for five seconds to stretch the jaw muscles. Close and let the jaw hang loose and slack. There will be a gap between the upper and the lower teeth.

Induction: Open the eyes widely, breathe in. Breathe out and close the eyes. Then pace with your breathing the following suggestions two times each:

1. *My eyes are firmly closed, firmly closed*
2. *My cheeks are warm, cheeks are warm*
3. *My lower jaw is passively hanging, passively hanging*
4. *Arms are heavy, arms are heavy*
5. *Belly breathing is slow. Breathing is slow*
6. *Legs are heavy, so heavy.*
7. *I double my relaxation from top to toe by taking a deep breath.*
8. *I go to my favorite place, favorite place.*
9. *I focus with all my senses on every detail and I enjoy my pleasant experience.*
10. *I orient to my body, feeling good.*

The step number 8 means dissociation between body sensations in the present and mental experiences of another time and place where you can experience colors, shapes, sounds, touch, feelings, smells, and tastes . Enjoy! When a positive feeling is strong you could suggest hand levitation and anchoring of feeling by pressing hands against the cheeks. When you later press on your cheeks the good feeling will come at once as a so called conditioned reflex. Practice self hypnosis daily until bruxism has ceased.

As a help to remember the steps you could make a drawing representing the different body parts involved from the eyes to the legs. The first three are situated in the face, the next three you can remember if you think the first letters of the alphabet A, B and of L representing the lowest part of the body.

18. Hypnosis for children

Children have a rich imagination and often live in their world of imagination or in a playful world. Most children enjoy tales and get into the trance if they are told with insight and understanding of the child's current needs. Most induction methods used in adult hypnosis also work for children. The most important thing is to get the child interested and cooperative. As an introduction to hypnosis one can ask, "Do you like animals?" Then you find out what kind of animal and then you suggest an imagination where the animal is involved. It is important to constantly help the child to make the chosen image as clear as possible. Below is an example. Other topics may be about movies, games, sports, interests, etc. Originally the animal in the example below is a white rabbit, but it is wise to choose an animal that fits to the child's own experiences.

Do you like your dog? What is the name of the dog? -Jack. Would you like to close your eyes and pretend that he is here, sitting or lying on you? Do you feel how heavy he is? Do you like having him there? Good! (If the dog is too heavy, use magic transformation). *You can hold your hands so Jack does not fall down* (show) *Jack likes to lie like that. You can feel a little on the coat. Jack is quite calm and you too. He'll make sure you're doing well and I treat you and your teeth well. Now, Jack and I want to look at your teeth, so I want to open your mouth and put your jaw in a comfortable position, if you please help to open up? There. Let it stay there. Very comfortable! I can see a hole in a tooth. Jack thinks it smells strange. He thinks it would be a good idea to clean it and then fill with some white material. Is that okay with you? I use a funny machine that whistles and sprays water.*

(Run the highspeed for a second or two and touch a tooth surface with it). *Jack sees how it splashes water and I think that you like that the smelling hole is cleaned. I spray a little more water and remove dirt. There you go. Now I'm digging with another machine to make it really clean. It's like a small digger that removes the rest of the dirt from the tooth. Jack looks interested.*

Children who do not want to cooperate of course have a reason for this. It's important to show respect by finding out how they think. At the same time it is important to get them to understand why they need help and why they need to cooperate if you make reasonable demands. Sometimes the child can be resistance minded. You should not force it to anything. However, the resistance must be broken, at least symbolically. You can for example offer the noncompliant child to get acquainted to the chair by just touching it and then come back another time. However the condition remains, that the chair should be touched with the hand. If a parent is present, he/she often helps with persuasion, as the claim seems to be most reasonable.

A child who is determined to make resistance does not accept any form of cooperation and with this attitude there is risk for continued resistance. While persuasion is ongoing, the therapist has the opportunity to show understanding of the child's behaviour and find out what it is based on, what the child thinks is at risk. As with adults, whatever may be the basis for the resistance this should be clarified and calming promises should be given. It should be made obvious that you offer full control, pain free treatment and no holding. A fairly common experience is having been hold firmly. Of course, one must be able to promise not to use violence or force.

Preparatory training at early age of children to get acquainted and familiar with dental staff and equipment care means a lot to create a positive attitude to dentistry. You can teach the child to shut the eyes and relax while blowing with the blister and spraying in the mouth. Giving positive fantasies and giving the child a good experience makes a good start. Small children often want to investigate by feeling and touching. Like a game with the drill, draw a happy mouth on your own thumbnail and then possibly even on the child's.

Sometimes the little child wants to sit in the parent's knee. Let them and offer them to tell a little story if they just shut their eyes. The main purpose is to get the child used to the environment and to have the eyes closed and listen to you. When they are closed start to tell:

A little anxious rabbit came with his/her mum to a dentist. The mum called her little child her bunny. The dentist was very kind. The bunny was allowed to sit with his/her mum in the dentist's chair and then the bunny was offered to look at all the instruments. The mother was asked to sit on another chair. The dentist showed a kind of vacuum cleaner and a water spray and asked the bunny if he/she knew how a water pistol was working. The bunny was allowed to play with the dentist's spray that resembled a water pistol and was not afraid anymore. So no you may open eyes and I'll show you how my instruments work.

Show how the water spray works and tell about how it is used. Ask the child if it's okay to let the mother sit in another chair while you show your other instruments and machines. When the child has been shown as much as possible the next step, including trance, is described in a positive way. Then you give praise for today's progress and give a small reward.

It should be borne in mind that a suggestion needs time to work. Therefore, after the fairy tale, which certainly puts the child and perhaps the parent in trans the good emotional atmosphere this has created make desensitization and positive conditioning to the environment possible. It is not important to go any further than demonstrating things to the child. Many dentists are performance-oriented, but in the above case, one should bear in mind that pressure can create back pressure and destroy what is aimed at. Only if the child seems to be fully prepared for a dental treatment it should be performed and preferably under hypnosis.

From a psychological viewpoint it is very valuable for small children to visit and be acquainted with a dental clinic and with hypnosis. They can be taught to relax with eyes closed and be used to the operator spraying water in the mouth. Evoking positive fantasies and giving the child a good experience is a good start. Small children often want to investigate by feeling and touching things. Like a game with the drill, you can draw a happy mouth first on your own thumbnail and then possibly even on the child's. A reward from a treasure chest could mean a lot to the positive attitude towards dental care.

The actual hypnosis induction is usually very easy to make, if you have first gained the trust of the child. The same principles apply to both adults and children. What differs are the methods. The child does not care about the therapist's reputation, status or other form of prestige. It's influenced by being shown respect, and by being taken seriously and if the dentist takes time to listen and answer to questions.

An induction of hypnosis should in general be very short because children go very easily in trance. You may have noticed how good they are at pretending when playing with dolls or weapons. Children love phantasy and magic. If a therapist is talented in these areas that can be useful, provided that the child feels safe in the situation. From six years of age children are excellent subjects.

In general, induction should be very short because children have a good imagination. When they play different kinds of games it is obvious how easily they can pretend in role playing. An induction that suits most children is the TV method.

Do you have any favorite film, video, game or Tv-show? Now I want to show how you can pretend to see it here. Take a deep breath and shut the eyes when you breathe out. Up here you can see a screen, can't you? Good. Now choose what you want to see. When the picture is clear, one hand raises a little. Good, there it comes. Look what is happening on the screen! It may be very exciting. When I place your hand on the armchair you will continue to look at the screen. Everything feels comfortable and you are doing well.

19. Deepening and maintaining the trance state

Regardless of the degree of suggestibility, there are different ways to consolidate and deepen the emotional state of consciousness that hypnosis represents. Below is a list of deepening methods. Preparedness for emotional commitment is promoted by shifting between calming and engaging stimuli. One can for example use a monotonous voice combined with suggestions of calm, rest and relaxation and contrast with an engaged voice that promotes curiosity and dedication. In order to maximize the subjects attention, you can also use some loaded words like "reveal, a secret, exciting" etc. Physical touch also attracts spontaneous attention.

The shift between experiences based on calm and relaxation and emotional excitement, narrows attention, and increases focus. This can then be used to deepen the relaxation which is important in dental treatment. Monotonous stimuli and suggestions of passivity and calmness increase an activation of the parasympathetic nerve system, which usually is the preliminary goal. A strong focus also means dissociation or in other words strong barriers against disturbing stimuli.

Dissociation means a cleavage so that several processes in the brain can go on simultaneously without disturbing each other. There is a barrier between the conscious perception of suggestive effects and the part of mind that has received and accepted the suggestions. Hypnosis means functioning reflexively, without carrying out conscious influence and control. In suggestibility tests, consciousness is focused on the experience of suggestions becoming realized and the mechanisms that are behind are unconscious and the cause of the effects is dissociated. This may be observed when a posthypnotic suggestion is realized. If you have suggested a behaviour and ask why it is performed, you will almost never get the correct explanation, but instead a typical rationalization. Humans have a clear tendency to overestimate logic as an explanation to their own behaviours.

Deepening methods
1. Constantly focusing on the heaviness of arms or legs deepens automatically over time.
2. Monotonous suggestions of increased depth, calm, relaxation, and comfort. You can also give non-verbal suggestions in the form of monotonous strokes or massage with the patient's allowance.
3. Finger levitation together with suggestions of deeper relaxation in other parts of the body.
4. Alternate between calming, relaxing suggestions and fascinating experiences of ideomotor, ideo sensory or cataleptic responses.
5. Fractionation. Make subject go in and out of trance and suggest more depth each time. Dissociation between the waking state and the trance state deepens.
6. Strengthen dissociation between the unconscious force that makes a suggestion work and the conscious experience of its effect. Example: Is it not it strange that your finger moves without you making any effort?
7. Amnesia. Example: Backwards counting and the suggestion that the numbers will disappear. An indirect method is when a conversation topic, started before treatment, is picked up immediately after trans and thus tend to make the patient forget about the entire treatment. This requires deep trans.
8. Confusion methods. Examples: a) To count down for the sake of ending trance then suddenly change direction and count upwards again together with deepening suggestions. b) Using strange words or sentences that are hard to understand like: "Understanding that a

standing, standing <u>over</u>, standing <u>under</u> or standing <u>for</u> makes understanding of standing different but now you only need to understand the importance of relaxing mind and body. So, relax!

9. To visualize something and activate as many senses as possible. Example: golf course, nature, human or animal, happy occasion, holiday memory, walk, hobby activity.

10. Creating association to ongoing event. Examples: You go into a deeper relaxation when a) your arm is sinking, b) the chair is lowered. c) I have opened your mouth and put the jaw in a comfortable position, d) I count to ten, e) you breathe out, f) you imagine going down on an escalator, g) riding an elevator or walking a stairway downwards. You can associate deepening to practically anything.

11. Dissociation between what is going on in the imaginary world and in the reception room. Example: "You are in a favorite place. In another place and time you are at the dentist, but that's something that you don't need to focus on. Soon your right hand will start to move upwards as a sign that it is numb. You may stay in your favorite place and focus on what is going on there. When the hand reaches the cheek the numbness will leave it and go into the cheek and stay there. Then the hand goes down automatically. Being able to be in two places at the same time is possible because of so called trans logic, free from critical evaluating. However the different situations should be held apart as much as possible and be looked at as two films running simultaneously on different screens.

After deepening, you may want to know the result. You can ask for this and get it confirmed in many ways, but it is important that the answer is not consciously made. Finger signaling can be used or an imagined thermometer, designed to measure trans depth.

Special techniques for deepening

ABC technique according to Elman, suitable for dental care
Though you're relaxed, maybe you'd like to relax even more? The deepest

state of relaxation you can reach in three steps. The first we can call level A, which is twice as deep as right now. Then there are two more levels, B and C where C means total relaxation.

When I say A, your relaxation will double and then say A. When I say B and it is doubled again and you say B, etc. In a moment I'll ask you to take a deep breath and when I say A you release the air, double the relaxation and say A. Are you prepared?

Breathe in! A, let out the air, relax. – A.

Breathe in! B – B. *Good – and then you take a deep breath and breathe out when I say C and you'll reach the deepest and most comfortable level of relaxation.*

C – C. (usually barely heard) If nothing is heard, suggest a finger signal instead.

An alternative to breathing is an imaginary ride in an elevator from a floor plan A down to plan B and C.

The escalator

Deepening of relaxation is easily associated with a downward movement such as going down an escalator, going down in a lift or a regular stairway. After the initial relaxation, the escalator is a simple and effective deepening method. Dissociation is involved so you will talk to two separate parts. Example: You are now relaxed, but I think you can reach a much deeper level of relaxation. Do you want to test? Just follow my instructions: *Feel how relaxed you are and at the same time prepare yourself for a deeper state. Imagine standing above an escalator and seeing the grooved steps moving downwards in a long line. You may see the black rails as well? When I count from 10 to 1 you will go down. Meanwhile your relaxation here will be doubled. When I say 10 you tread the escalator, enjoying the journey while I count. 10. Enter the escalator and hold the railing. 9. Down, standing up, going down 8. Going deeper. 7. Deeper 6. You sink deeper 5. Now halfway down, deeper relaxed. 4. Just enjoy it. 3. Continuing down. 2. Almost down. Much more relaxed. 1. Get off find a comfortable chair and focus on the pleasant feeling of relaxation. Continue to relax.*

The five rooms

Demonstrated in Stockholm 1972 by Gerald E. Halker, DDS

When relaxation has begun after a hypnosis induction, the following deepening method is an option that is easily associated with the idea of going deeper into oneself. A house often has psychological associations related to the own personality.

When relaxation has begun after an induction of hypnosis, the following deepening method is an option that is easily associated with the idea of going deeper into the inner world. A house has often been shown to represent the own person.

Imagine a house with at least 5 rooms. You are outside the entrance. In order to be able to enter, you must be at least somewhat relaxed. The key is to let all the little muscles around your eyes relax until the eyelids are completely relaxed, feel firmly closed and won't open. The eyelids are firmly closed and comfortably relaxed and won't open.

Now you can enter the house and look at room no 1. Each time you enter a new room your relaxation will double. As a signal to enter room no 2, I'll count to three. At three, open your eyes, close them immediately, double relaxation and enter room no 2. Are you prepared? 1,2, 3. – Good! Are you in room no 2? How many windows are there? Now you will have to proceed to room no. 3 in the same way to get twice as relaxed again. 1, 2, 3. – Is there anything on the walls? Though you're comfortable, you can go for even deeper relaxation. Continue to room no 4. One, two three. Lovely. There is a lot of interesting things, but the most interesting is the deep relaxation that comes automatically when you come into room No. 5. This time, when I count to three, you must relax completely around the eyes so that the eyelid can not be opened when I get to 3. This will give you the key to get into room no 5. – 1, 2, 3, eyes firmly closed, totally relaxed, enjoying the calm feeling and there are dreamlike sceneries waiting for you while work is done. A finger will raise by it self to give me a sign that I may start.

Depending on the treatment to be performed, appropriate suggestions are given after which treatment is commenced.

20. Hypnosis and CBT in collaboration

Cognitive behavioural therapy has had great success, mainly because treatment results have been documented and therapist are educated to adhere only to evidence-based treatments. An important insight is that problem behaviours are acquired through learning and can be influenced by the same learning methods that once caused them. To the letters of the term CBT should actually be added the letter E for emotion. The physiological expressions of emotions may rather be considered as reflexes than behaviours. For example, autonomously regulated palpitation, perspiration and altered blood pressure could preferably be called reflexes.

How to clarify the automatic negative thoughts behind experienced discomfort or negative mood in cognitive therapy is already described. Conscious training in realistic thinking gives results. Another way of influencing is the method of conscious self-suggestion launched by Coué in the 1920s. Some modern therapists work with positive affirmations that work in the same way as Coué's conscious self-suggestion.

CBT and hypnosis have a lot in common. Some emotional disorders are seen as a result of negative thinking and harmful behaviours, both within the CBT and in the hypnosis discipline. Working with relaxation and alternative thinking, as done in CBT, is effective in most cases of dental phobia. The new and desirable behaviour for patients in dental care is often relaxation, which can be greatly facilitated by induction of hypnosis. New ways of thinking are also facilitated if they are practiced under hypnosis. Then, automatic, positive thought- and behaviour reflexes can be suggested to replace the negative ones without any conscious effort.

Cognitive therapy, founded by Aaron Beck in the 1960s showed better results than the ordinary psychodynamic treatment at that time. Combined with behaviour therapy hypnosis makes treatment more effective and faster. By conditioning, one can make sure that desired thoughts and behaviours are triggered in a reflexive manner. Kirsch's (1995) meta analysis provides a clear indication of increased therapeutic effect when CBT is combined with hypnosis.

Measurable responses, not regulated by the autonomic nervous system can be divided into three categories:
- Operant-conditioned behaviours that are governed by rewards and punishments or expectations of such.
- Automated behaviours occurring by slentrain because they once have been chosen for good. They are maintained by unconscious perceptions, which are not questioned. These include, rituals, security behaviours and behaviours that are practiced until they are performed automatically when initiated. Traumatized individuals can develop automatic trance states.
- Behaviours that can be termed ideomotor activity. Such is elicited and governed by focusing on imagined performance of muscle activity. Such behaviours are typical of trance states. It is spontaneous and influenced by unconscious impulses. The body language is largely shaped by ideomotic activity.

In CBT exposure is a standard treatment of unwanted, operant-conditioned or automated behaviours. In dental care, a person with needle phobia may hold a syringe in his hand and examine it until discomfort has subsided. Thereafter, the operator may suggest a role play where he pretends to put anesthesia but the needle should be covered and the patient's role is to open mouth and then be passive and not even frown. The important thing is to make sure the patient does not make any movements of avoidance or grimaces.

This exercise causes anxiety, as soon as the syringe with the covered needle is brought into the mouth. The move from outside to inside the mouth must be repeated several times until no reaction is visible. The next step is pushing toward the intended injection site with the plastic hub covering the needle. After getting used to this a patient probably will accept that a drop of anesthesia is placed on the mucous membrane with a very light pressure. The surface will get anesthetized whether it is perforated or not. After a while a few drops of anesthesia can be injected painlessly. The goal of the whole procedure is to make the patient abstain from any kind of movement to be able to learn that the injection is acceptable and must not be feared.

21. Hypnosis and pain relief

The standard induction or any method to make the patient become re-laxed may be used. When relaxation is satisfactory, proceed according to the following example:

Example 1
You do not need to focus on what I do and I don't need to know if the tooth that I am going to work on is alive or not, as long as you feel comfortable. You must not bother about anything and I promise to be as careful as I can. Imagine that this area of the hand is disconnected from the brain and that the feeling is gone. The skin may be like a thick leather and the hand like a foreign object of wood or plaster. Or it may feel cool as a sign that it is anesthetized. Your index finger will raise as soon as you notice the change. Relax and imagine that your hand is a dead thing, stunned, insensitive.

Now your finger feels lighter, it is automatically beginning to raise as you relax away the feeling in the hand. (Pinch the hand). *You notice that the harder I'm pinching the more you relax.* (Pinch harder) *It's like dead material, numb! The feeling is gone. The fingers continues upwards and the hand gets lighter. Soon the whole anesthetized hand will float up. Higher and higher. It moves towards your face. When it reaches the lip or cheek, the anesthesia will move over there. Almost there! Now the anesthesia passes into the lip, the hand becomes heavy and sinks down and you notice that your lip (cheek?) is numb. It feels different! I'll guide your arm down to the armchair.*

The numb feeling goes deep into the jaw through teeth and gum. The teeth and the gum here (show) *are numb. As a sign to me that I can start my work, an index finger will lift. If you want me to pause, just take your finger down.* (When the finger has come up): *Well, now I help you to put the lower jaw in a position where it it feels comfortable and it can stay there.* (Place the jaw so that the mouth is wide open. The patient may need to help). *Keep this position exactly. It feels increasingly comfortable. You breathe calmly and relax more and more during treatment. Perhaps your thoughts automatically go to some positive memory?* Observe and comment on reflexes. Encourage deep relaxation, passivity and calm and mention the possibility of distraction by focusing on some pleasant memory rich in detail.

Comment: The above mentioned, somewhat detailed induction is only recommended in exceptional cases, primarily for patients who have never previously had hypnosis and who are particularly worried about pain but don't want chemical anaesthesia.

Example 2
When relaxed, pain sensitivity is reduced. Imagine that the nerve conduction from this part of the jaw to the brain is interrupted. It may look like a colored string which is cut here somewhere. (show) *Try that image! Notice what happens when the image is clear.* Test!

Example 3
You are now so relaxed that your thoughts are free to go far away in time and space. You can go for a round of golf, be on holiday or be in any pleasant place you can think of. Make your choice and when you are there, this finger (stroke) will come up as a signal to me that I can do my work here. You can always stop me by lowering the finger.

Example 4
When listening to music with a strong beat you can feel the rhythm in your body. It is likely that your foot or head may move rhythmically. You can certainly remember some music that you like. If you focus on it until you feel the rhythm I would like you to let your forefinger move up and down with the beat.

As long as the finger moves rhythmically it is a good indication of dissociation strong enough to eliminate pain without any specific suggestions given about it.

Headache
Tension headache is common and can be an obstacle to hypnosis induction if you do not treat it. Sometimes the patient asks for an analgesic tablet. Then you can offer to begin the session with treatment of the headache. An effective way of dealing with it is to work with so-called sensory modalities and their submodalities. By this is meant different ways of describing with the help of metaphors and examples, especially from the visual sense. The pain can be visualized as a coloured area and you could ask for a description of colour, shape, and range. Are the boundaries sharp or diffuse? After this description the suggestion is given to look for changes. It could also be effective to give the direct suggestion that the colour will change to another one. Such a change should be repeated at least three times and then relaxation should follow.

Some patients describe their headache by using a special sensory submodality They may talk about weight, hard steel ribbon, pressure, or a pulsating feeling in an area surrounded by a soft membrane. You should notice what kind of expression the patient prefers and use words from the same submodality. Just the imagination sets limits.

What usually happens is some kind of change for the better and then you can give relaxation suggestions to the subject that usually has already entered a hypnotic state. After completion of dental treatment, the headache will be gone. The method has been launched by representatives of neurolinguistic programming, NLP. The authors are Richard Bandler and John Grinder. They studied the successful therapists' working methods and then launched their theories.

Patients who are helped are, of course, happy and grateful. Sometimes they want treatment for other problems, eg migraines, asthma, IBS (irritated bowel syndrome), etc. As long as a dentist or hygienist stays in his field of work and teaches relaxation and hypnosis, it is good if this also helps the patient with other problems. However, care should be taken not to treat problems for which there is no education and the right competence.

22. Nausea reflexes

Nausea reflexes are caused by muscle tension and strong focus on discomfort. The treatment consists of relaxation and careful and methodical desensitization. There may be many different psychological causes. As a dentist or hygienist you should not, without special education, undertake to investigate these in detail. One can explain to the patient that if he/she is completely relaxed and at the same time pays attention to something else it's impossible to choke. You can also explain the principles of desensitization and make an exercise with successive approximation and the patient deeply relaxed.

Example 1
After an induction of hypnosis ending up in good relaxation, proceed as follows:
You are now relaxed and calm. If you could see yourself from outside, you would see a person looking perfectly relaxed and calm in the dental chair.

Imagine seeing yourself with mouth open and that you do not react at all when a mirror is held against your tongue. The good feeling of complete calm is there all the time. I would like you to see this as a movie and when you see the mirror in the mouth let your index finger float upwards. As long as you feel calm the finger should stay up. About 30 seconds is all that is needed, but if you get tensed stop the film and lower the finger immediately. – Good now you've done it and can take down your finger.

Now, see the same scene and I'll demonstrate how good you are at re-laxing when I touch the tongue with the mirror. I'll wait for a signal from your index finger that I can go on. (Try the mirror one second and praise for the relaxation. Increase the time gradually). *Now that you've done this you can become even more relaxed when you experience a nice memory of a place you like.* (Work calmly and methodically constantly aiming for new successes)

Example 2

The patient gets a nuisance when an X-ray is taken. There is no time for any long hypnosis induction, so just get full attention, direct it away from the oral cavity and give suggestions in a firm voice. *This is not working! We must try another way. Do just as I say! I'll show you how. Stretch your arms parallel, straight forward so that your palms face each other.* Keep your fist in the middle and say: *Imagine my hand is a magnet that pulls your hands against each other. Continue to imagine that my hand is there working like a magnet.* Remove your hand and make suggestions that the hands are pulled against each other. When they are at a distance of hand, you quickly push them together, put them down and say in a loud and firm voice): *Relax! Deeper, feeling more comfortable and calm. Feeling calm. Now take a deep breath through the nose. Relax when you exhale. Swallow and the sensitivity is gone when you open your mouth.* Insert the film and and take the X-ray without hesitation, without delay, but in a gentle way. Sometimes it is easier if the operator holds the film.

Example 3 (after Gerald E. Halker, D.D.S., USA)

Have the patient with retching problems stand straight in front of you. Hand a mirror and suggest him to see how far he can put the mirror into his mouth. If a reflex comes say: *Oops! You really have a problem. Do you want to get rid of it? OK! Look at my finger!* Hold the finger straight in front of your nose tip. **Take three deep breaths!** Look intensively on the patient's right eye all the time and after the third exhale say immediately and with the greatest conviction: It's better now and you can test for yourself, though there may be some left. Let's try to put the mirror in your mouth and certainly it will go better. Then proceed:

Do you know why it's not quite good? You did not breathe deep enough and you didn't swallow after each breath. Do you want to get rid of the problem completely and forever? Alright! Please sit down. Now, look at my finger. Take three really deep breaths. Look for signs of fatigue in eyes and surprise by closing them with your left hand's thumb and index finger while giving suggestions of relaxation both verbally and through strokes from the shoulders down to the hands. Check the relaxation and, if necessary, deepen for maximum relaxation. Then proceed: *All right, from now on, your retching problem is gone and will not return. It doesn't exist. As easy as a bad habit can start as easily it can disappear.* Have the patient demonstrate that it is no longer possible to retch.

23. Spontaneous attention is influenced by words and conversation topics

If the patient is tense from the beginning, everything that is said or done will be interpreted in the light of previous negative experiences. Then it's important to reduce the number of negatively charged words to a minimum and instead use positive, security-creating words and behaviours. Examples of words that should be avoided have been mentioned before. Words that can be recommended are: nice, relaxing, calm, easy, warm, successful, free, good, perfect, excellent. Each word helps to direct attention. Therefore, you should be generous with positive words that can be referred to as interspersed suggestions.

If one feels uncertain about what the subject's imagines when giving suggestions it is advisable to give several options. Deep relaxation may be perceived as heaviness or a floating sensation. Body parts that feel heavy won't move but a floating sensation may lead to movements and levitation. If you have observed i little movement after suggesting relaxation and heaviness you could continue: *Feeling heavy or feeling a floating sensation may indicate relaxation. The body parts that feel heavy won't move. There was a little movement in your right hand. Is it going to move or will it relax and become heavy when you go deeper into relaxation? Now there was another little jerk. Maybe the movements is a sign that a floating feeling is about to develop in the hand. Then it may be felt like a piece of wood held under a water surface.*

Usually a levitation will start. If no more response is visible, suggest heaviness only.

Particularly important is the choice of words during induction of hypnosis. Everything that is said and done should have the common purpose of directing the subject's attention to the next goal of the induction. Even if the main goal is relaxation the next goal may be limb catalepsy. Then words like heavy and relaxed should be spared until later. Even the tone of voice, the whole body language should be coworking in helping the subject to focus on the right things. Minor hesitation or an unsecure tone can activate the critical thinking, which should be avoided. People are more affected by how a message is conveyed than by its exact meaning.

Attention should be paid to behaviours that promote hypnosis, such as the subject not taking any own initiatives, not changing position, being relaxed and passive, breathing slowly and responding to suggestions. Praise is important and it should be given immediately when the kind of behaviour that you want is observed. The art of knowing when to be silent is very important. Sometimes it may be obvious that the patient is in the own inner world and comments would be unnecessary and disturbing to the hypnotic state, also called trance..

Some people with high prestige, such as doctors and professors, do not always know much about suggestion and therefore may make statements that work as suggestions. When patients are anxious to hear what the doctor says they are very susceptible to suggestion. If somebody hopes to get a positive message but the doctor uses the word incurable this may work from the unconscious mind in the future. Even if better better medicines appear the negative suggestion "incurable" may worsen the prognosis and be a hinder for cure. Neither the patient nor the doctor are aware of how detrimental a negative suggestion may be for the health. At best, the statement is positive like: "This medicine will help you".

Thus, be careful with words and think of what the Swedish poet, Alf Henriksson has written about them, here in free translation from Swedish:

A word that a person takes special notice of
may exert influence for unpredictable time.
It can bring joy to the end of life.
It can cause discomfort for the rest of life.
Thus – words affect life on earth,
so be careful when using words.

The main influence of hetero-hypnosis is usually made via the language. Words trigger imaginations and emotions stored in the unconscious mind. Therefore, the language should be used with aforethought for making effective, deliberate and positive impact. The American Milton Erickson was a master of this. Below are some examples of how he used the language to facilitate the flow of unconscious thoughts to take a special direction tol facilitate a particular purpose:

Intension

Promote passivity.

Wording

You do not need to listen to me.
The important thing you will still hear.
You do not have to do anything. Just relax and enjoy. The breathing takes care of itself.
You do not need to know how to deepen relaxation. Abdominal breathing starts automatically when relaxation is deepened.

Pay attention to autonomous responses

Your breath is slower now. As the body relaxes, a calm picture may pop up. You know that the brain can solve problems even when you sleep. Experiences come automatically when you are

deeply relaxed. It's hard not to relax in a comfortable chair. Heaviness means relaxation. What
do you think you would feel in a deep hypnosis?
(Repeat subject's words!)

Stimulation of spontaneous associations

You have had interesting experiences in your
life. You are free to experience what you want.
Perhaps some memory pops up? When looking
back you can rejoice in positive memories. You
can forget things consciously, yet know that you
know. The brain works best when it can work in
peace and quiet. Memories can be about scent,
taste, feelings, color and sound. Children have
strong feelings. Getting attention means a lot to
them. It may feel unreal when a finger lifts automatically. A face that meant a lot can be remem-
bered. It has to do with emotions. A golfer has
the goal clear before each stroke. Details are
best seen in close proximity. Nature can provide
strong experiences

Preparing for ideomotor response

Reflexes are not guided by willpower. A finger
that moves automatically may surprise. A piece
of wood held under water flows up to the surface
if released. Your index fingers are completely free.
Which one will lift when you feel ready? You can
nod your head as an answer to the question: Are
you relaxed? I wonder if you head will nod if I
ask: Are you in a trance?

Preparation for ideo sensory response

A numb arm may feel like a foreign object. The
heat of the sun may feel good on bare skin. On
a hot day a cool breeze in the face is refreshing
When you are deeply relaxed, parts of the body
may become disengaged from the brain. The
feeling disappears. Teeth become like dead wood.
Neither you nor I need to know if your teeth have
a feeling or not. But you can pretend they are
stunned, disconnected from the brain, numb.

24. Communication, motivation and rapport

Preparing for hypnosis and taking a leading role has to do with communication. Before induction of hypnosis, the therapist should establish a good relationship, a consensus combined with a mutual trust, called rapport. The ability to create rapport is a natural talent in most, but can be improved in many ways. It is important to become aware of how to communicate and what to communicate. A large part of the communication is via body language, which in turn is largely influenced by thoughts and emotions

The first contact is important. Discomfort should held at the lowest level possible from the first moment. In order to succeed, it is wise to think about what may cause anxiety and try to minimize that before treatment. Many patients feel more secure if they have the same operator year after year. In lack of that, they may feel safer if they know the premises or at least any other staff working in the place. As soon as a new patient has arrived, someone should take note that they have arrived and be welcoming. A health declaration that contains the issue of discomfort should be filled in. If there is a delay this should be reported in order to prevent unnecessary worry and tension. It takes about 20 minutes for stress hormones to break down.

Patients who report discomfort or fear of dentistry should be given the DFS-form. It is good to draw attention to the different aspects of their problem and it gives the operator an image of competence, particularly important to new patients. Taking fear and discomfort seriously is appreciated and brings confidence and motivation for cooperation that are very important at induction of hypnosis. An interview that records previous experiences is usually very popular. However usually only a very short report from the patient is needed.

The creation of rapport is about empathy, understanding and attempts to see common values. It is therefore important to pay attention and adapt to the patient's main opinions, body language and language pattern. The notion of pacing is precisely about this and especially about adjusting breathing to a common rhythm when inducing hypnosis. Most important is a positive attitude, empathy and a safe appearance.

In all communication in dental care the sense of security successfully transmitted by the operator is important for creating rapport. Many patients feel reluctant to be in the treatment situation, and some may have thoughts of avoidance, flight or defense and are on guard. By showing acceptance and understanding, the important rapport can be established for successful treatment. If an operator has high prestige, it will make it easier. With prestige, this means that you are recognized as proficient in your professional role.

The content of the verbal communication may be chosen to enhance rapport. Often, the patient communicates already at the first contact something that means a lot to him/her and therefore is in the consciousness. The operator who actively listens captures this and may make it a conversation topic that makes the patient feel noticed and confirmed. If the message is: "I had problems with my new car" this could be the conversation topic.

Sometimes communication is about the weather and then there usually is also extraverbal communication embedded. It could be about being open for communication or about the own emotional state. With this insight, it is understood that as an operator, you should not primarily emphasize your own thoughts about the weather but instead show interest in the patient's feelings. Another way of creating a positive climate is to give a compliment for clothing, oral hygiene or anything else noticeable.

Motivational psychologists have looked at the needs that guide us in different situations. The so-called organic needs must be met before the rest can claim. They have to do with the most basic needs like hunger and thirst and protecting against bodily harm. Worrying causes anxiety, an emotional motive which in turn leads to a need to resort to someone who can give a sense of security. The operator who, through his body language and speech, can give this sense of security while giving guarantees against physical damage has laid the foundation for a good rapport.

As the social beings we are, we have an unconscious need to define in the meeting with others how the relationship should be defined. You can choose between different ways to relate to others. Adult- adult relation means showing that one responds to each other as two equal individuals. Such a relationship is called symmetrical. In different situations the need for new roles arises.

A teacher-student relationship is called complementary and may be appropriate for a hypnotist-subject relation. However, it should be preceded by accurate information about what is planned and then an adult-adult relation is the best. Another type of relationship in contact with patients is parent-child and this should mostly be avoided. When giving instructions in oral hygiene, the instructor can easily end up in the parenting role with the patient in the childhood role. A sense of shame can be awakened and it can distort the message. Communication in this case is unilateral between the sender and the receiver. The patient feels bad instead of listening to well meant suggestions and only remembers being blamed.

In all communication between people there is a continuous evaluation of who will hold the leading role. For a hypnotist it is necessary to have the patient accept a subordinate role, even if the usual role in the working place is being the boss. Patients who have difficulty in subordinating often signal this clearly by being impatient and demanding. Often they sit with their hands clasped and their thumbs up, which according to body language experts specialists can be interpreted as wanting to dominate.

Verbal and nonverbal communication should be consistent and unambiguous. Those who have just begun using hypnosis are advised to practice their induction method until no uncertainty is observed. A tone that reveals doubt or uncertainty creates confusion. The spoken word must not be contradicted by the body language, the non-verbal language.

Creating rapport means getting in touch with a person. The patient's needs should constantly be regarded. Therefore, it is important to observe and read the body language. You have to be flexible in taking different roles. To gain rapport the mirroring (imitating) of body language is effective and also being able to trace thoughts and feelings. You should know when it is time to shift from pacing, another word for adapting behaviour to the patient's, and take the role of a leader. During hypnosis induction it is important that the roles are evident and accepted.

When explaining the purpose of a planned relaxation instruction, an adult -adult relationship is preferred. However, when it comes to hypnosis the patient should accept a subordinate role. The operator is the leader like a teacher or a secure parent. Attention is guided by emotions and expectations, and hypnosis means positive ones, i.e. a parasympathetic reaction. Many patients feel a certain tension in the dental treatment and they need support and safety. To be clear about what you want to do and to radiate peace and evoke desire to cooperate provide good conditions for practising hypnosis.

Flexibility is good. Some patients want you to carefully describe what you intend to do. Others do not want to know anything. There is no absolute truth, but you can judge case by case and ask patients how they want it. Some don't want to lie down and then they should be allowed to sit up. Certainly it may be uncomfortable to the operator, but if the patient re-laxes sitting, you can tempt into accepting a somewhat tilting position by suggestions of even more comfort when leaning the backrest. If you do this gradually the patient usually accepts a lying position when relaxed.

25. Preparing and implementing hypnosis in dental care

1. A certain fear in the patient may facilitate contact with an understanding dentist or hygienist and this is positive for induction of hypnosis. If the fear is at a very high level, it must first be reduced, which usually takes about 20 minutes. The adrenaline content in the blood has to drop to a reasonable level until relaxation is possible.
2. Explain why a brief introduction of relaxation can help, and ask for permission to show how to relax in just a few minutes.
3. Hypnosis induction. All techniques aim to focus the patient's attention by providing some sort of mission so that the number of outer stimuli is reduced and muscular activity is limited. The focus is usually turned to the experience of relaxation and weight. Monotony and positive suggestions are often enough to get a satisfying relaxation.
4. Deepening usually occurs automatically after a short hypnosis induction or relaxation aid, which may be a better wording. Suggestions for relaxation and calm and a comfortable feeling are always given and this is often enough. The main issue is that the patient is motivated to linger in the good feeling that relaxation gives. Many deepening methods are based on that the patient's attention is varied, e.g. by alternating between giving a test and then suggestions of rest in a monotonous way. One of the most useful tests is finger levitation.
5. Often desensitization to fear provoking stimuli is required. Desensitization can be about tolerating drill sounds or vibrations, accepting

instruments in the mouth without nausea and vomiting. Analgesia is to be provided either by injection or by suggestion and distraction.

6. Occasionally, disturbing moments bring the patient out of trance. This is quite normal, but you should ensure that a return to deep, comfortable relaxation takes place. It usually comes back very quickly. Switching between normal consciousness and hypnosis can be deepening by promoting dissociation between the two states. This technique is called fractionation.

7. Post-hypnotic suggestions are those usually given at the end of a session and intended to be realized after the completion of the session. Compliment the patient for what has been good and suggest that it will be easier and easier to relax during dental treatment. You can make ego-strengthening suggestions if you think there is a need for them. They can be about being balanced, beeing healthy, calm, sleeping well, enjoying life, brushing the teeth regularly, etc.

8. To terminate trance after completion of treatment under hypnosis, including possible post-hypnotic suggestions, make it clear to the patient that the treatment is complete and that it is time to come out of the relaxed state and to activate themselves. Stretching of arms may be suggested. No special ritual is necessary but giving the patient a little time to orientate themselves while you wash your hands is appropriate.

9. Immediately after trans, the suggestibility is very high. You should therefore be extra careful about what you say and do. You should not show signs of stress or harassment. Before the patient walks, make sure that the patient is not absent minded. The attention should be directed outwards and no suggestions, if not wanted should remain. However, this is unusual.

It is usually best to do the hypnosis induction at the beginning of a session. It's a good idea to offer all patients a few minutes of relaxation and induce hypnosis provided that the patient is positive. The purpose should be clarified, i.e. giving a so-called rational, a logically based motivation

135

for why relaxation is good. The word hypnosis does not need to be used, as it often awakes false expectations.

Sometimes, during treatment, you may notice that the patient strains the muscles in the hands or face. It may also be seen sweat drops in the forehead or on the upper lip. Such signs should be regarded as an indication of tension and thus a need for hypnosis. Report your observations and that you would like to take a few minutes out to show how to lower the tension. A suitable induction method often starts with focusing on signs of tension, e.g. standard induction with focus on catalepsy and stiffness in the arm, or the hand clasp test.

In general, patients often have a certain degree of concern and tension before treatment. This makes them highly susceptible to calming suggestions of relaxation as a natural sedative. Therefore, a slight worry and tension can be turned into deep relaxation. If there is severe anxiety and associated tension, it may be difficult to influence with calming suggestions straight away. Often it is easier if you first strengthen the tension locally, draw attention to it and then provide suggestions for peace and relaxation. The hand clasp test or the catalepsy in rigid arm are appropriate.

26. To end trance. Post-hypnotic suggestions. Anchoring

When you as a therapist are done with the dental work, you can let the patient understand this and expect it to function as a signal to go out of trance. Most patients usually orient themselves in space and leave the state of the state without any remaining effects. It may still be appropriate to ask if it feels good. It may happen after deep hypnosis that there is a tendency to slip back in trance. In that case, it is important to provide suggestions that counteract this.

Counting loudly from 1 to 5 or vice versa is a common "waking" procedure. If you do, you should be consistent and always count the same for both your own and the patient's sake. I usually prefer to just say the treatment is done and it's time to rinse the mouth. It then seems more natural than always using a wake-up procedure. Another reason for not "waking up" is that it is good if the patient can go in and out of trance in a simple way during treatment. Getting out of trans is not more remarkable than leaving a cinema after a moving film.

If the word sleep has not been used, it may seem inappropriate to use the word wake. Instead, one can talk about shifting focus and of activating oneself after a pleasant repose. Sometimes it may be appropriate to ask the patient to stretch the arms as a way of activating the body. After the hypnosis has been completed, do not make anything that may cause discomfort. The suggestibility is, at the very most, immediately after the end of trance.

Post-hypnotic suggestions are those that are intended to work for the current session. It is appropriate to give them just before ending the hypnosis. If this has not been deep, one can not count on great effect of post-hypnotic suggestions. They can be about how oral hygiene is going to be pleasing and interesting, how new thoughts will replace old ones and then it's a good opportunity to praise for good cooperation. Although, as a therapist, you can feel proud of having succeeded in getting the patient relaxed, be careful not to praise yourself instead of the patient.

Ego strengthening suggestions are used to make a person think positively and feel good. According to the inventor of cognitive therapy, Aaron Beck, in the case of depression three things are of major importance. Of course, they are also important to everybody. They are about how to look at oneself, the surroundings (the world) and the future. Therefore, it is usually valuable to provide suggestions that strengthen a person's self-image, pointing to what is positive in life and opportunities that make the future brighter. However, you don't have to give post-hypnotic suggestions. Do it if you think it is appropriate.

A patient who experiences comfort and relaxation while hearing the operator's calm voice automatically associates the voice mode with relaxation, i.e. relaxation becomes a conditioned reflex triggered when the therapist begins to speak in a certain way. An emotional response can be linked to any signal presented while emotional strength is close to its peak. In NLP (Neuro Linguistic Programming), the therapist may touch the patient's arm or shoulder when the emotion is strong (anchoring) and can then trigger the same feeling at any time only by touching the same place and uttering a few words in a calm voice.

If a patient, despite the completion of the treatment and despite the fact that this is made clear, and suggestions that it is time to come out of trance and leave the chair have no effect, don't worry, take it easy. The best thing is to ask why they don't follow your suggestions? The answer will probably be something like it's so nice. Then it is usually effective to inform that the next patient is waiting and blow air in the face with the blast.

27. Deviant behaviours; possible reasons and explanations

In dental care you meet all kinds of people. Their origins, backgrounds and experiences have had an impact on them and thus underpin their worldview and behaviour. Some behaviours can make a therapist very upset if they are seen only as expressions of nonchalance, neglect, insanity, stupidity, defiance, distrust or ingratitude.

If you as a therapist are upset, it may be reassuring to try to understand both the own reaction and the causes of the patient's behaviour. The person who has grown up under normal favorable conditions may have expectations that those who have not had a good start in life can never live up to. It's wise not to judge too hard or be too categorical in one's conclusions. However, you must make reasonable demands and set limits.

The first year of life has a big impact on how the rest of a person's life will develop. There are basic needs that must be satisfied to ensure healthy development. John Bowlby has shown that a safe bond to a caregiver in the first year of life is of great importance and that the lack of such often leads to future problems. Even if there is a caring person some babies are thought to be more vulnerable than others. Maybe this is about suggestibility? If they have to wait too long until their needs can be satisfied the stress may become intolerable. The result may be lifelong feelings of insecurity or aggression.

When finally a caretaker arrives, the feeling becomes very strong. The child learns to perceive existence as either terrible or positive, but has difficulty in perceiving that one and the same person can awaken both kinds of feelings. They usually switch between either only seeing bad sides or only the good ones. In their emotional thermostat there are no intermediate positions. There is no communication between the different states that exist. The phenomenon is called cleavage, a form of self-defense mechanism typically for persons with diagnosis of borderline, nowadays called emotional instability.

Another early defense mechanism is denial. When a toddler has happened to smash something to break apart and says: "it was not me" is an example. Infant's feelings are strong and change between lust and unease. The need to protect itself from unease is inborn. When eventually an awareness of the own self develops over the next years, a need to defend a positive self-image is developing. It is so important because a negative one gives strong unease, as it can be taken as a sign of not being loved.

Psychologically there are many ways to defend self-esteem. Mistakes can be blamed on someone else. If you get late to the dentist, it's easier to put the blame on others or circumstances that are out of your control. The truth that you should have started earlier is seldom heard. Mor often the excuse ares like these: "The bus was late, I got stuck in a car queue, my car is in a garage and was not ready as they had promised, my child got sick." Avoiding to see your own flaws by seeing them in others or blaming other than yourself is called projection.

Aggression searches for outlet, but in some contexts it may be risky to express it. Then the need to ease the pressure can be satisfied by showing aggression against anybody else. A person who is angry with his boss may let his anger trubble his family. Fear and anger are controlled by the same hormone and can easily pass into each other. A scared patient can get outraged in front of a dental nurse when she announces that the dentist has been delayed, but then turns out to be shy and forgiving in the treatment room.

Early, one learns how to hide what you really feel in social contexts. One learns to lie in order not to cause discomfort to others. Instead of saying the truth, one might say something that means quite the opposite. A boss can say to a subordinate that he would not do without him but actually mean that it would be nice if he would quit. However, unintentionally, signals of disregard are sent. The dual messages lead to discomfort and uncertainty among those exposed to them. Although so called white lies are sometimes needed, there are times when honesty is best. Criticism can be expressed in a friendly and constructive manner.

Rationalization implies a need to explain actions with logically founded and socially acceptable arguments. Buy of expensive new cars is usually officially motivated with sound reasons like crash safety, strong motor for safe overtakings, quality etc. If there are much cheaper cars with proof of the same safety, even higher quality, and engine strong enough seems to be irrelevant even if the price would be the half. You seldom hear anyone say that the most important reason was a will to impress on the neighbor. Some dental clinics focus on patients who need to show to others that they go to a luxury practice. There you can expect a beautiful facade, high prices, focus on selling expensive dental care, whether needed or not, and rarely cheap, simple solutions. Of course you may also find really good dental care in some of the luxury and expensive clinics.

In children who have a special orientation, the requirement for order and discipline can develop into obsessive-compulsive disorder. Performing of the compulsory acts can be very time consuming. The compulsion can also lead to the development of fixed ideas. Once they have been firmly rooted, they are very difficult to handle. Anxiety symptoms have often by the affected been mistakenly interpreted as evidence of amalgam disease or allergy. Attempts to convince that there are other explanations sometimes causes a lot of discomfort, which leads to strengthening of the fixed idéa, i.e. the explanation lacking evidence.

It becomes especially difficult when a patient requires healthy teeth to be pulled out. The reason given for this may be that once these teeth had amalgam fillings and even if they have been removed, the patient thinks that there is a poison left that causes him/her to feel sick. Absolutely absurd reasons are stated and the dentist who is not willing to stand up for the patient's demands is in disgrace. Unfortunately, there are too many who respond to the patient's requirements, even if it leads to mutilated occlusion and only gives a short-term lowering of anxiety.

Since the oral cavity from a psychological point of view, is an important and private zone, dental treatment can cause negative emotions and also positive ones. Briskly telling the patient to open the mouth and then inserting a mirror and probe can create very negative emotions. It is better to approach carefully and make sure that there is an agreement of what to do and when.

Patients who have been subjected to abuse or other traumatic experiences may see in the dentist or hygienist a person with similar quality as the one who commits abuse and then be overwhelmed by acute and severe anxiety leading to discontinuation of treatment. However, this is very rare. Dental therapists should be aware that they are persons of authority. To the extent that parents or other authorities have in some way made a strong impression, the same emotions are easily aroused by other authorities like dentists or even dental hygienists. Then it's extra important to keep calm and give the patient the chance to discover who you really are and what you stand for.

Suddenly appearing anxiety that is perceived as a lightning from clear sky is called panic attack. The one at a high level of tension is at risk of an attack especially if it has happened before. During the attack it may be so difficult to get air that death agony is felt. Dizziness and pains from the heart region increase the fear. Those who know something about panic attacks and realize that the patient has suffered from this can be very helpful through accurate information and a calm behaviour. Reducing the main stress level, information about panic and training in rapid relaxation are among the measures that have been shown to cure the attacks.

28. Case reports

Acute pain in wisdom tooth
Despite having got a lot of anesthesia the patient experiences pain when attempts to extract the a wisdom tooth are made. The operating colleague notices the patient is worried and tense and thinks that the pain experience is psychologically conditioned. I am asked if I could help with hypnosis. I accept and is presented as an "expert" on dental surgery and dental ansthesia. I add another small dose of anaesthesia, most in order to demonstrate that I take the pain experience seriously. Then I ask for permission to make the anaesthesia as effective as possible by using hypnosis for relaxation purposes. The patient looks at me with horror shining in her eyes asking me what I'm going to do. I answer that hypnosis is deep relaxation and that concentration is required.

Clasp your hands and I'll show you! The patient puts the palms against each other and I decide to instead of hand-clasp test suggest that the hands are glued together so that the palms feel like they are glued together as if they were two pieces of wood. *They are stuck,* I say a few times. Then I say that **when I grab the wrists the hands will come apart and the arms immediately become heavy and relaxed.** A few minutes later, the tooth is removed, the patient is amazed but happy and felt no pain.

Tartar removal

Despite signs of discomfort, the patient says that it does not hurt and does not want anesthesia. I say that even if it does not hurt it will be more comfortable if you could relax and offer to demonstrate that. After some hesitation, I get an approval to spend a couple of minutes on a short relaxation exercise. When I intended to put an arm on the armrest during standard induction, it became cataleptic and rigid at halfway. I let it stay there and suggested that the hand was resting on arm rests on a floating pillow that would soon start to sink. Suggestions ot arm heaviness were given it the hand and arm sank gradually and when the arm landed was completely relaxed. The rest was shear pleasure.

I have contacted you because I am so extremely afraid of dental treatment. I have a dental infection that needs to be addressed as soon as possible! Just the knowledge that I have to do something "bigger" in my mouth soon makes me very stressed !! I actually do not know how to handle it. I was at a dentist in October and he gave me a soothing tablet (Stesolid) that I would take before extraction of the tooth. I would rather not drug myself and I also feel that it would be better trying to get rid of my fear instead of just "stun" it temporarily. I have been very afraid to go to the dentist for as long as I can remember! That, in combination with the fact that I've always had a lot of problems with my teeth, has made the fear turn into a big anxiety that I'm struggling with daily.

"I'll describe a little what I think is hard for me; I'm NOT a person afraid of pain. (I've recently had a baby and it went well, ha ha ?!) What I think is the worst is the feeling of losing control. I hate the feeling of being anaesthetized as it makes me quench and a feeling of swelling in my throat and difficulty in breathing! Then it's also very hard to have many instruments in my mouth and I can also get a nuisance and panic of it (especially of a canvas attached to a tooth, (for example at root filling). I also have a fear that something will fall into the throat. This has happened to me once when the dentist was scared and pulled me up in a sitting position. One might say that I'm a bit of a control freak. What I wish is, to be able to carry out surgery in the mouth and succeed in being RELAXED and let the dentist do his job in peace and quiet! I do not want to be a troublesome patient anymore! I am aware that I have much that needs to be done in my mouth and I really want to do this now soon! Another problem is that I am afraid of heights. I sincerely hope I can get help!"

Diagnosis and treatment:
Diagnosis: Severe dental fear, fear of heights, excessive need of control.
The fear of heights was treated with imagined processing of submodalities. The fear was felt like a big handball in the diaphragm. The surface was said to be smooth. The ball could be shrunk. Progressive relaxation was administered. Eyelids moved. Finger inquiry about the cause. Want control. Backwards counting plus the word deeper and suggestions to forget the numbers. Empty consciousness and relaxed eyelids. Glove analgesia was practiced. Gapträning. Suggestions to tolerate instruments in the mouth. Explained that the important thing is that the operator reacts to signals and interrupts directly on the agreed signal. Anchorage of good feeling from positive episode of life was made. Stroking from shoulder down to hand was used. Posthypnotic suggestion to be able to relax at the dentist. Gave a signal that the treatment was complete!
After opening of the eyes the right arm felt stunned. Asked me about the reason for that. I explained that I had only suggested this phenomenon in her hand but that she probably had thought of anaesthesia when I stroke the arm with my hand. A test of height phobia showed that it was under control. Pat. ordered dental care and the problems disappeared all at once.

Isolated at the infection department after dental treatment
Diagnosis: Extreme dental fear
Anamnesis: A dentist scratched open mouth ulcers which appeared after a smallpox vaccination. The patient then got smallpox and was isolated in a hospital. In this, she saw a connection with the dental treatment and has ever since avoided dentists. She does not know why she's so scared,

but can't bring herself to go to a dentist. There is often pain in the teeth, causing panic feelings. On such occasions, she has been able to seek a dentist. Five years ago, such a visit was made after a period of pain after a tooth repair that failed. It ended with extraction. It was unpleasant to lose a tooth. The reason she is now coming for a consultation is that she has been accompanying some patients of mine in her work and then she has become somewhat accustomed to the idea of herself coming here.

Treatment: Emergency treatment of a painful teeth. After chemical anesthesia induction of hypnosis followed and then there was no trace of fear and a root canal could be carried out and completed in the same session. The following session time was devoted to discuss the causes of the fear and making the patient realize that she was wrong in some respects. She also learned to realize that dental treatment does not have to be uncomfortable, especially if you go for dental care on a regular basis. After another couple of visits with dental treatment during hypnosis, the patient claimed to be cured from her horror.

I have always been afraid of the dentist
The patient became frightened at the age of 7 when she had to change her dentist to someone who was tough and unpleasant in general. Also later, she has had to change dentists many times. She is not afraid of pain but experiences the environment in a dental surgery as very unpleasant. This has meant that she has not been able to go to the dentist for the last ten years other than when she has very acute pain. At the last dental visit, a tooth was drawn due to pain and swelling. The dentist was unpleasant and just talked about my bad teeth.

There were plans to cancel the appointment with me despite the knowledge that we would not see in my dental surgery. At the initial consultation a short hypnosis induction was performed with good results. Dental treatment could then be carried out without any problems.

29. Self-hypnosis, self-expression and self-knowledge

It is not necessary to be particularly susceptible to suggestion and hypnosis to become a good hypnotist. For self-hypnosis, however, you need to know how susceptible you are to suggestion and choose the method accordingly. About 70% are sufficiently susceptible to benefit greatly from self-hypnosis. In today's society where the tempo is high be careful not to stay at high levels of stress to long. Relaxation by means of self-hypnosis can do wonders.

When you have found your way to deep relaxation it may be useful to train rapid relaxation, that you can use as soon as you feel unnecessarily stressed. You may also need to exercise to remain relaxed for a certain amount of time, ranging from ten seconds to hours. When relaxed, you can practice self-esteem by looking at the image of yourself as you want to be. Another way is to repeat a certain phrase, a so-called affirmation to achieve a particular purpose. Above all you should try out an efficient way of inducing self-hypnosis.

A good way of doing it is to speak something appropriate to yourself on a tape/smartphone and then listen to it. An induction that I use myself sometimes is the relaxation instruction in Chapter 11. To be able to do it without help I then omit certain moments. At the end, I focus either on a harmonious place, a lake from my childhood or on one of my many sailing or flying trips. Sometimes it ends with a calm, harmonious feeling combined with deep relaxation. Here is a description of a short induction of self hypnosis. After each of six deep inhalations, the following self suggestions is focused on, one by one at the exhalation.

1. *Close your eyes and relax on your face.*
2. *Relax the neck muscles*
3. *Relax in your hands and arms*
4. *Relax in the stomach and back*
5. *The legs may become heavy and relaxed*
6. *Relax from top to toe*

When you feel relaxed, you can decide to leave the relaxed state, activate yourself by stretching and then exercise quick relaxation. When prepared, *breathe in deeply, exhale and relax. Remember the feeling of deep relaxation, focus on it and you'll be back in that state.* Stay for at least 10 seconds, preferably longer. At another occasion your level of tension, on a scale 1-100 may be as high as 70. If it can be reduced by 20 units to 50 within a few seconds, this is valuable, even if it is just a reduction of tension. Then you can use the technique of lowering tension every time when there is a risk of unnecessary tension.

When relaxed, it is also advisable to exercise selective relaxation. One can for example lift an arm while keeping the rest of the body relaxed. As soon as you lower your arm, it should relax. It may be good to think through the stresses you experience during a day and maybe you could avoid some unnecessary tension. If you get too tense put small stickers in the places where you should relax. It can be at the phone, at the computer, in the car and in the bathroom. In CBT this is called applied relaxation. For those who suffer from panic attacks, quick relaxation is particularly important. The attacks can be prevented from occurring.

There is research showing that migraine patients who, when they feel that an attack is coming, can stop the attack if they succeed in getting their hands so relaxed that they feel warm. Hands getting warm is a phenomenon that has to do with relaxation. This is a fact discovered by the German psychiatrist Johannes Heinrich Schultz, the inventor of Autogenic training. It is a method of self-suggestion in a systematic way. You spend time relaxing, sitting or lying comfortably and start by thinking repeatedly: *I'm very calm.* When you have practice this you add a new suggestion about once a week. The second week you repeatedly think the words: *I'm calm and my arms are heavy.* The third week: *I'm calm, my arms are heavy and my hands are warm.* The fourth week: *I'm calm, my arms are heavy, my hands are warm and my breathing is calm.*

Further suggestions are: *The heart beats quietly and steadily, the forehead is cool.* In addition to these, suggestions about feeling of weight in the legs and the whole body may be added. Weight suggestions are repeated about 6 times and calm 3 times. Once this has been practiced, Schultz has added a further training phase that has the character of meditation. As a theme, color, shape, sound, words, people, self and inner reality are used. For each of these themes there are spontaneous associations that can provide deep trance experiences. It can thus be seen as a form of self-hypnosis or meditation.

Positive psychology is on the rise today. It has gathered ideas from how to deal with problems of different kinds. Life should not only be about being free from illness and mental problems, but also about wellbeing and enjoying life. Most people have understood that exercise is important. Excessively high level of stress is an increasing problem in the modern society and it can lead to a psychological burn-out. Pauses are important, relaxation gives a possibility to load the batteries and therefore it is really a health-promoting behaviour.

It is important to find the right balance in life, to know yourself and your needs. There must be a balance between excitement and relaxation, work and leisure, duty and pleasure, solitude and togetherness, happiness and seriousness, sense and reason, just to name a few examples. One should have fun at work. The one who directly in the morning thinks of what kind of positive things that await during the day feels better than the one who begins the day by saying, "Oh no, today will be a boring day of work."

When relaxed, you can use so called affirmations to foster positive imaginations and cognitions. They can consist of a few short sentences, preferably with rhyme. Examples:

My goal is clear. I have no fear.

I trust my ability to provide well for my family

In the morning I'll say, this is my day

Sleep I'll find, by relaxing my mind

In my work I come into play, I'm happy every day

My meal is small. Sometimes I don't eat at all

Affirmations don't need to be rhymed. If you want to find more affirmations, seek on the internet at:
https://www.prolificliving.com/100-positive-affirmations/

Self-awareness
A way of self-knowledge, Freud felt was interpretation of dreams. Obviously there is a lot of symbolism in dreams. Freud differentiated between manifest content and latent content. The latent often has an emotional theme. The only one who can tell what it is, is the dreamer himself. A good way of working with a dream is to go on feeling until you get an association to any situation with similar emotional content.

An easy way to acquire self-awareness is to work with guided affective imagery or symbol drama according to Hans-Carl Leuner. It is about 10 standard images that are used as starting points for fantasy excursions in the inner landscape. You learn to understand that it's not just a coincidence that controls the choices you make when you are asked to imagine something. As a test image, one uses a flower. It is easy to believe that the choice falls on a flower that has recently been seen, but it is rarely what determines. Since the flower is included in my standard induction of hypnosis, I will go into the symbolism

Leuner emphasized that emotions are involved and strongly affect the images that appear. As far as the choice of flower is concerned, it is certainly interesting which flower you choose, but even more interesting are the characteristics attributed to it. It is common to ascribe the flower qualities that are ideals to oneself. A successful, somewhat noisy, confident person who received the flower test saw a rose. It was a powerful, fresh rose that grew in nutritious soil.

Another more modest, but equally successful person saw a small violet growing in a rocky cave. It had windshield, but was well accessible to the sunshine. The landscape was barrenright, but the flower was brightening up, clearly shining. The description was in line with the appearance that the person gave. The image works as a projective test, but is not used as such in the dental context. Group participants who want to get to know each other, can do this quickly by present their flowers with their respective characteristics.

Another similar, less standardised test using images has been launched by the American Joseph Shorr. Those who want to increase their self-knowledge, may be interested in knowing the existence of this kind of tests. Here are some examples of suggestions for images: 1)An animal comes out of your head. What do you see? If you are that animal, what do you do? 2) You are within a circle. What do you see, feel, do? 3) You are affected by two forces, etc. The number of pictures is infinite and after testing a number, one notices that they say a lot about oneself.

30. Ethics

In the United States, the law states that the patient must be informed and give his/her written consent to hypnosis. It is fortunate that this is not necessary in Sweden. An agreement to use relaxation is enough if that is the main purpose. Relaxing and maybe dreaming away for a while usually people takes as a natural thing and rarely defines it with the word hypnosis. By avoiding the word, you do not evoke false expectations. You just want to teach the patient to appreciate their own ability to relax instead of focusing on the therapist's role. After a successful hypnosis, one should give praise to the patient.

To practice clinical hypnosis causes close proximity to patients because emotions arise during treatment. As a person using hypnosis, you often experience great gratitude and trust. However, one should try to prevent patients from becoming too tied to one's person and should strive for them to feel free and dare to change to another dental clinic if necessary. The trust you have gained should be managed well and always put the patient's best interests in the forefront.

No matter who is a patient, you should always do your best to provide optimal treatment. One should only work with hypnosis within the area of competence and be prepared to refer to legitimate professionals with valid treatment skills if psychological treatment is requested. If you charge for hypnosis the cost should be settled in advance. Be honest, about what training and competence you have. Especially important is to be truthful when you advertise.

If the patient is treated elsewhere, avoid questioning of the advice given there. If you are critical, it is better to contact the other caregiver to sort things out. The problem can be high-dose anxiety drugs, where a reduction or a termination sometimes is needed to get the best effect of hypnosis treatment. In some cases the tablets may only be taken for safety purposes and in that case it is an unfavorable so-calle safety behaviour.

In some countries, bodily touch is taboo. For ordinary Swedes, it's generally okay if the therapist is touching an arm or a shoulder. The way to do it, as well as the purpose, is absolutely crucial to whether it is ethical or not. If there are any doubts, the rule applies that there is an informed consent about the type of treatment offered. However, it does not have to be in writing. If it is a treatment that is unusual and if you feel the least doubt, you have better to make a note in the journal that the patient is in complete agreement.

When working with relaxation and suggestion, you may accidentally cause unpleasant memories. Be means of tensing muscles of the neck, shoulders and jaws, unpleasant memories can be kept away from consciousness. During relaxation, unwanted memories can become aware. The patient can get a lot of trouble which may lead to discontinuance of all contact. Well, this rarely happens in dental care, but if it should occur then the operator should be prepared to comfort and calm. It is then important to let it take as much time as needed to comfort.

There are cases where sexual exploitation has occurred. Such is as illegal as taking care of someone who is deported and defenseless. Those who exercise hypnosis have a moral responsibility.

31. Interior design and outfit of the dental clinic

Although the most important for dental patients is to be met with kind treatment, the environment is also important for their well-being and expectations. A bright and spacious waiting room with comfortable, relatively high chairs is usually preferred by most patients. Tension is common in the majority of them and psychologically they are not prepared to allow themselves to sink down into low and soft chairs even if such furniture is supposed to be relaxing.

Newspapers should be up-to-date and chosen because they should work to attract attention, offer distraction and gladly discuss interesting dental issues. Ev. music one should preferably be able to influence by turning off, muting or selecting an option. Noise from treatment rooms shouldn't reach the waiting room. Colors and materials should be carefully planned so that it is obvious that the intention is to please. Living plants create a positive atmosphere if they are fresh and well-kept. Artwork is hard to say anything definite about except that there should be no scary motives in a waiting room.

The toilet needs to be looked after so that there is no blood stains or splashes after someone who has an extraction and may have left stains of blood. Often, patients who arrive go straight to the toilet and the first impression is important. It's nice if there are mugs for those who want to drink water. Inside the treatment room as little instruments as possible should be visible. Letting the patient have probes, syringes or dental instruments in the field of vision is stressful for some. The ideal from a psychological point of view is to keep the field of vision free of instruments, at least initially.

On the roof you can put some beautiful posters with neutral motifs, preferably beautiful nature pictures. Many patients are used to listening to music. It's hard to know what kind of music would have a calming effect, so let them choose for themselves. Providing luxury headphones is appreciated by many. In fact, if you present the possibility of listening to music as a way to relax and disconnect pain, it can sometimes replace a hypnosis induction.

Literature

Aron, E. *The Highly Sensitive Person* (2013) Kensington Publ. Corp.

Bandler, R., Grinder J. (1979) Frogs into Princes. Neuro Linguistic Programming.Real People Press

Baudouin, C. (1921) *Suggestion and Autosuggestion: A Psychological and Pedagogical Study Based.* London: Forgotten Books, reprint 2013.

Benson, H. (1976) *the Relaxation Response.* New York: Avon books

Björkhem, J. (1939) *Det ockulta problemet: en orientering.* Uppsala: Lindblad.

Coué. E. (1967) *Self Mastery Through Conscious Autosuggestion.* London: Allen.

Erickson, M.H., Rossi, E.L. (1979) *Hypnotherapy. An Exploratory Casebook.* New York: Irvington Erickson M.H., Rossi, E.L., Rossi, S.I. (1976) *Hypnotiska verkligheter. Klinisk hypnos och former av indirekt suggestion.* Stockholm Natur och Kultur.

Erickson M.H. (1967) *Advanced techniques of hypnosis and therapy.* Selected papers. Ed. J. Haley. Grune & Stratton Cop.

Erickson M.H. m. fl. (1961) *The practical application of medical and dental hypnosis.* New York. The Julian Press.

Ewin, D.M. & Elmer, B.N. (2003) *Ideomotor Signals for Rapid Hypnoanalysis: A How-To-Manual.* Illinois: Charles Thomas Publisher.

Frost. T.W. (1959) Hypnosis in general dental practice. London: Henry Kimpton

Gerge, A. (2013) *Hälsofrämjande kommunikation.* Stockholm: Insidan.

Gerge, A., Rosén G. red. (2011) *Klinisk hypnos vid smärtbehandling.*

Haley, J. (1973) *Uncommon therapy. The psychiatric techniques of Milton Erickson, M.D.* New York: Norton & Company.

Hartland, J. (1971) Medical and Dental Hypnosis And Its Clinical applications. London. Baillère Tindall

Le Crohn, L. (1977) Selbsthypnose:Ihre Technik und Anwendung im täglichen Leben. München: Goldmann.

Leuner, H. (1985) *Lehrbuch des Kathatymen Bilderlebens.* Bern: Verlag Hans Huber

Leuner, H. (1984) *Symboldrama.* Stockholm: Natur & Kultur.

Mason, A.A. (1960) *Hypnotism for medical and dental practitioners.* London: Secker & Warburg.

Meares, A. (1961) *A system of medical hypnosis.* New York. The Julian Press, Inc.

Milechnin, A. (1967) *Hypnosis.* Bristol: John Wright & Sons Ltd.

Norrsell, N. (1972) *Odontologiska synpunkter på klassisk betingning.* Tandläkartidn. 64: 404-407.

O'Donohue, W & Krasner L. (1995) *Theories of behavior therapy.* Washington, DC: American Psychological Association.

Öst, L-G (1987) Applied relaxation:description of a coping technique and review of controlled studies.Behav. Res. Ther. ;25(5):397-409.

Watson, J.B., Rayner, R. (1920) *Conditioned emotional reactions*

Wolpe, J. (1954) *Reciprocal Inhibition as the main basis of psychotherapeutic effects.* Archives of Neurological Psychiatry, 72: 205-226.

Wolpe, J. (1958) *Psychotherapy by reciprocal inhibition.* Stanford, CA: Stanf. Univers. Press.

Wolpe, J. (1995) *Reciprocal Inhibition: major agent of behavior change.* In W. O'Donohue & L. Krasner (Eds.), *Theories of behavior therapy* (pp 23-57). Washington DC: American Psychological Association.

Shaw, S.I. (1958) *Clinical applications of hypnosis in dentistry. Philadelphia* W.B. Saunders.

Schultz, J. H. (1967) Übungsheft für das autogene Training, konzentrative selbstentspannung. Stuttgart : G. Thieme

Uneståhl, L-E. (2012) *Coaching med mental träning: den ideala kombinationen.* Göteborg: B4Press

Uneståhl, L-E. (1982) *Hypnos i teori och praktik.* Örebro: Veje

Wirstam, H. (2014) *Metakommunikation.* Stockholm: Vulkan

Young, Klosko & Weishaar (2003), Schema Therapy: A Practitioner's Guide. New York: The Guilford Press.

Index

.